Witchcraft in Early Modern England

Witchcraft in Early Modern England

James Sharpe

An imprint of **Pearson Education**

Harlow, England · London · New York · Reading, Massachusetts · San Francisco · Toronto · Don Mills, Ontario · Sydney
Tokyo · Singapore · Hong Kong · Seoul · Taipei · Cape Town · Madrid · Mexico City · Amsterdam · Munich · Paris · Milan

Pearson Education Limited

Head Office:
Edinburgh Gate
Harlow CM20 2JE
Tel: +44 (0)1279 623623
Fax: +44 (0)1279 431059

London Office:
128 Long Acre
London WC2E 9AN
Tel: +44 (0)20 7447 2000
Fax: +44 (0)20 7240 5771
Website: www.history-minds.com

———————————

First published in Great Britain in 2001

© Pearson Education, 2001

The right of James Sharpe to be identified as author
of this work has been asserted by him in accordance
with the Copyright, Designs and Patents Act 1988.

ISBN 0 582 32875 6

British Library Cataloguing in Publication Data
A CIP catalogue record for this book can be obtained from the British Library

10 9 8 7 6 5 4 3 2 1

Set in 9.5/15pt Stone Roman by Graphicraft Limited, Hong Kong
Printed in Malaysia, LSP

The Publishers' policy is to use paper manufactured from sustainable forests.

For Pyewackett
Too Dim to be Demonic

Contents

Preface

It seems that every month brings with it a new book on the history of witchcraft: a work of synthesis, a regional study, a book exploring a new interpretation of the phenomenon, a newly edited version of a demonological text. The subject is one of ever-growing complexity, one where professional historians, working on sometimes intractable court records or on difficult and massive printed works, are constantly challenging the assumptions about witchcraft held by both non-specialist historians and the general public. Most of this research centres on the period of witch persecution in the late middle ages and the early modern period, let us say between about 1450 and 1750. Much of this work is concerned with continental Europe (scholarly work on German witchcraft in particular has experienced something of a renaissance recently), while the flow of publications on the trials at Salem in 1692 seems unending. The aim of this book, appearing as it does at such an exciting point in witchcraft studies, is to provide the reader with a short introduction to the history of witchcraft in early modern England, focusing especially on the period when witchcraft was a secular crime, conviction for which might lead to execution, that is between 1542 (or, perhaps more meaningfully 1563) and 1736. Experience as a university teacher has convinced me of the need for such a book.

Because of this, I am envisaging that the main readership for this book will be undergraduates, although the tendency for witchcraft to be taught in sixth-form history courses, and to provide the basis for Advanced Level project work, has made me aware of a readership in schools. It seems likely that most of the students reading this book would be taking history, although it may well also be of use to students of English literature, and would also help provide an historical context to students studying witchcraft in a number of other disciplines, notably women's studies and anthropology. I would also hope that this book will be of use and interest to anybody requiring a guide to the history of witchcraft, especially of witchcraft in England.

The geographical and chronological structure of the book has already been made clear. The thematic structure is dictated by an attempt to examine some of what the general consensus among historians would consider to be the main approaches to the subject. After a brief introduction in which some general themes are raised, the first chapter is focused upon how witchcraft looked to people who were in positions of authority (whether that authority was political, administrative, theological or cultural), thus illuminating what sort of ways of thinking about witchcraft might be open to the educated inhabitant of early modern England. The second chapter looks at what has been one of the major themes of English witchcraft studies since the early 1970s, the connection between local community pressures, neighbourly tensions, and witchcraft accusations and trials. Some of the issues raised in this chapter are carried on to the next, which consists of an exploration of some of the broader aspects of witchcraft as an element in popular culture. The fourth chapter addresses what is still one of the most problematic aspects of the history of witchcraft in England, and, indeed, in Europe more generally, namely that of the decline of belief in witchcraft, or, to be more accurate, that of a decline of witchcraft beliefs among the educated elite. There then comes an assessment where a number of threads are pulled together and reassessed, a selection of documentary extracts chosen to illustrate and support the arguments and interpretations put forward in the text of the book, and an up-to-date bibliography.

There is no other work offering the type of short, interpretative guide to the history of witchcraft in England which this book comprises. And although this book is concerned with a specific national experience, it constantly offers points of comparison with the history of witchcraft in the period it covers in continental Europe, Scotland (where the history of early modern witchcraft ran a very different course) and New England. It attempts to offer a state-of-the-art guide to the major interpretations of the subject, and to make the reader aware of the complexities of witchcraft as an historical phenomenon without becoming enmeshed with levels of complexity and detail which would be inappropriate to an introductory guide of the sort intended here. Above all, the provision of a collection of documentary extracts, many of them gathered from hitherto unprinted archival sources or from books and pamphlets which were published four or five centuries ago, offers the reader unusual opportunities to get a flavour of how the phenomenon of witchcraft was written, spoken, and thought about in England in the years between the mid-sixteenth and the mid-eighteenth centuries.

My appreciation of how a book of this type might be organised and written, and what documentary extracts might usefully be included in it, has been sharpened by several years of teaching a second-year course on the European witch-craze to undergraduates at the University of York. The writing of the book has also been facilitated by conversations with my colleagues Wolfgang Behringer, Mark Jenner, and Bill Sheils. As ever, however, my biggest source of support and encouragement has been my wife, Krista Cowman. The dedicatee walked over the keyboard of my word processor at certain crucial points in the authorial process.

Stillingfleet,
North Yorkshire.

Note on referencing system

Readers should note that numbers in square brackets [5] refer them to the corresponding entry in the Bibliography at the end of the book (specific page numbers are given in italics). A number in square brackets preceded by *Doc.* [*Doc.* 5] refers readers to the corresponding item in the Documents section which follows the main text.

Author's acknowledgements

I have attempted to use this book both to introduce the reader to the current state of thinking among historians about witchcraft in early modern England, and to provide a sample of the sources upon which any opinions about this subject must be based. In bringing this sample of documents together, I have drawn upon manuscript and printed materials held by the Borthwick Institute of Historical Research, York, The British Library, The Essex Record Office, Chelmsford, The J.B. Morrell Library of the University of York, The Public Record Office, London, York Minster Library, and The West Yorkshire Record Office, Wakefield. I am grateful to all these institutions and their staffs.

PART ONE

WITCHCRAFT IN EARLY MODERN ENGLAND

1

Introduction

Witchcraft and witch-hunting in early modern Europe are among the most written about, yet most elusive, of historical topics. Even before the last witches were burnt (as far as we know, the last legal execution came at Glarus in Switzerland in 1782), educated Europeans were trying to explain why the witch-hunts had happened. This intellectual quest has continued, for the era of the witch persecutions has never ceased to exercise a fascination for later generations. To the general reader, the witch-hunts retain two main characteristics. There is much about them which is bizarre, even laughable: one thinks of the belief in night-flying to the sabbat, of tales of sexual liaisons between witches and incubi and succubi, of stories about the talking demonic animals which were the witches' familiars. The knowledge that people in the past believed in such phenomena reassures us moderns as we attempt to maintain the notion that we live in a more rational age than did many of our forebears. Conversely, the fate of some of those accused of witchcraft was harrowing. Here, perhaps, one thinks of the letter which Johannes Junius wrote to his daughter as he faced execution for witchcraft at Bamberg in 1628, explaining that he had confessed to witchcraft only after being tortured so severely that even his gaoler begged him to admit to his non-existent offence to end his suffering [63 *p. 129*]. Or one could bring to mind the elderly and confused Janet Horne, the last witch to be executed in Scotland, warming herself beside the fire she was to be burnt on, thinking it had been lit for her comfort [64 *p. 78*]. Whether regarded as trivial and odd, or horrifying and inhuman, witch-hunting and the beliefs which underpinned it can all too easily be employed to create a possibly spurious cultural distancing between the past and the present. Indeed, the way in which witchcraft has so frequently been regarded as a metaphor for backwardness creates a massive barrier to the proper understanding of the phenomenon.

The European witch-craze: the main contours

Continuing research is constantly modifying our knowledge of the subject, but the main lines of what we might for convenience call the European witch-craze can be sketched with some certainty [65]. Ideas about witchcraft and magic had long been present in European culture, but it seems that it was some trials in Switzerland around 1400 which established the belief that witches were magical practitioners who owed their powers, which they used to do evil, to a pact they had made with the devil. This idea developed and became more complex as the fifteenth century progressed, so that it became accepted knowledge among theologians that witches were not isolated individuals dabbling in the occult, but rather members of a demonic, anti-Christian heretical sect. This formative period of the witch-craze was symbolised by the publication in 1487 of what is probably the best-known witchcraft tract to the general reader, the *Malleus Maleficarum*, written by the Dominican inquisitors Heinrich Kramer and Jacob Sprenger. But the publication of the *Malleus* was followed by a slump in witch-hunting, this being reversed in the post-Reformation period, when heightened concerns over religious conformity helped renew official interest in what were considered to be the devil's agents. Levels of trials and executions rose in many parts of Europe in the 1590s, and from then on there were serious epidemics of witch-hunting, notably in Calvinist Scotland in 1590–97 [64] and in some of the German Catholic episcopal states in the second and third decades of the seventeenth century [68]. By about 1630, however, scepticism about witchcraft was already beginning to manifest itself in educated circles in a number of European states, and over much of western Europe trials and executions were heavily in decline by the second half of the seventeenth century. There were, however, still some major outbreaks of witch-hunting, albeit in more geographically peripheral areas: Sweden experienced its one big witch-hunt in the 1670s, for example, and large-scale burning continued in Poland well into the eighteenth century. But by that date witchcraft was becoming an increasingly marginalised phenomenon for Europe's educated elites.

Explaining the witch-craze, as we have hinted, has been of considerable interest to later generations. The earliest interpretation, and that which is perhaps still the most widespread among modern Europeans and North Americans, is that the witch-hunts were the result of the ignorance, bigotry, and general stupidity of people in the past, and, more specifically, of the clergy and judges who were seen as the most active proponents of witch-hunting. The importance of Christianity in creating the witch-craze was re-emphasised by interpretations which stressed the impact of the Protestant Reformation and the Catholic Counter-Reformation, while the role of judges has been expanded into arguments about the relationship between witch-hunting and state formation. Other interpretations have centred on the rise of capitalism and the break-up of the traditional village community, and on witch-hunting as a by-product of patriarchy, misogyny, and the oppression of women. Rather less sustainable explanations of the craze have portrayed it as resulting from the effects of ergot poisoning following the eating of mouldy rye bread by the peasantry, from taking hallucinogenic drugs, or from the psychological impact of the arrival of syphilis as an epidemic disease. Moreover, concepts from other academic disciplines, notably social anthropology and psychiatry, have been borrowed to help interpret the historical phenomenon of witchcraft.

These theories and approaches owed much to non-specialist writers who formed their interpretations, which range from the incisive to the plain daft, on an imperfect grasp of the subject. Meanwhile academic historians, with a somewhat more sceptical attitude towards big explanations, were pursuing detailed and painstaking research on relevant source materials, attracted consciously or unconsciously to the premise that trying to get a better view on *what* happened might well be a useful preliminary to trying to explain *why* it happened. Obviously these historians, working as they have on different regions, on different printed works and court archives, and within different historiographical traditions, have achieved varying emphases in their findings [e.g., 51, 52, 53]. Yet in sum their researches have demonstrated that witchcraft and witch-hunting in early modern Europe were more complex phenomena than has generally been imagined, and that the most important consequence of this complexity is that no monocausal explanation for those phenomena is acceptable: the witch-craze is not reducible to the impact of a more aggressive Christianity, or of state formation, or of misogyny, or of the break-up of the village community, but rather of the interplay of these and other factors, with the nature of this interplay varying in different chronological and regional contexts. Moreover, and perhaps surprisingly, most of this research has tended to diminish the statistical significance of witch-hunting. Certainly, most previous estimates of the number of persons executed as witches have apparently been exaggerated, the once much-quoted figure of nine million ludicrously so. The current consensus is that 40,000 people were executed as witches in the period of the witch persecutions, between about 1450 and 1750. It is almost beginning to seem that the problem, given the pervasiveness of the factors which are normally adduced as having caused the craze, is to work out why there were so *few* witch-burnings.

Some key interpretations

If most academic historians would now reject monocausal explanations of the witch-craze, it remains clear that there are a number of explanatory perspectives which are generally acknowledged to be valuable, and these must now be outlined and contextualised. As we have noted, since the Enlightenment considerable emphasis has been laid on the contribution of the Christian church to the witch craze. There are certainly solid grounds for this. Most known cultures have accepted the existence of witchcraft or phenomena very like it, but it was the late medieval Christian church which created a specific image of the witch as a servant of Satan, as an enemy of God, as a being who had willingly joined the Devil's side in the cosmic struggle between good and evil. Modern reinterpretations of the history of Christianity in the late fifteenth, sixteenth and seventeenth centuries have taken a rather more nuanced view. The nineteenth-century rationalist's view of witch-hunting as the outcome of the activities of a bigoted, ignorant and persecuting church has now given way to one which stresses the cultural impact of both Protestantism and later Counter-Reformation Catholicism [e.g., 64]. A higher level of Christian knowledge and Christian conduct, a more engaged, active, and informed Christianity, were now demanded of the individual Christian. As the twentieth century demonstrated so vividly, this official stress on ideological conformity and higher behavioural standards helped create deviants. The witch-hunts which set in from the late sixteenth century can be interpreted partly as a by-product of those processes of Christianization which followed the Reformation, processes which, as the activities of Kramer and Sprenger demonstrate, were already stirring in the later fifteenth century.

The impact of these processes was made weightier by the arrival of what English political commentators of the period would have described as the godly commonwealth, and what modern historians have called the confessional or sacral state. Whatever else state formation in early modern Europe involved, the arrival of divine right monarchy and confessional absolutism meant that rulers began to take a heightened interest in matters religious, and that the good citizen became more closely identified with the good Christian (the type of Christianity in question was, of course, usually that prescribed by the relevant secular ruler). The connections were spelled out with some cogency by the foremost historian of Scottish witchcraft, Christina Larner:

> If there was one idea which dominated all others in seventeenth-century Scotland, it was that of the godly state in which it was the duty of the secular arm to impose the will of God upon the people... the new regime asserted its legitimacy by redefining conformity and orthodoxy, and by providing a machinery for the enforcement of orthodoxy and the pursuit of deviance. [64 *pp. 5, 41*]

In 1590–91 the king of Scotland, James VI, took a leading role in Scotland's first large-scale witch-hunt. In a pamphlet describing this episode, some of the alleged witches involved were portrayed asking the devil 'why he did beare such hatred to the king'. The devil answered, 'by reason the king was the greatest enemie he hath in the world' [35 *p. 15*]. Faced with such statements rulers, like James, with an enhanced notion of divine right monarchy would develop a very clear notion of where witches fitted into the broader scheme of things, and what ought to be done about them.

Relating witch-hunting to the activities of the Christian church or of the early modern state essentially presents a view of witchcraft 'from above', and is based on analysis of official attitudes as presented in the law code or the demonological tract. Rather less emphasis was placed by historians on popular beliefs about witches: indeed, one of the last scholars to write about the witch-hunts in the traditional post-Enlightenment mode, Hugh Trevor-Roper, declared that he was not concerned with what he described as 'mere witch-beliefs: with those elementary village credulities which anthropologists discover in all times and at all places' [75 p. 9]. From the mid-nineteenth century, however, the tradition grew that late medieval and early modern witchcraft was in fact a pre-Christian pagan religion, adhered to by the peasantry but attacked by the Christian church and the secular authorities. This notion was first formulated clearly by the French radical Jules Michelet in 1862 [67], but it was re-stated powerfully by Margaret Murray in her *The Witch-cult in Western Europe* of 1921. It was Murray's theories, reinforced by Gerald B. Gardner's *Witchcraft Today* of 1954, which laid the foundations of the currently fashionable view of witchcraft in the late middle ages and early modern periods as a coherent, pre-Christian religion. This idea, which is of central importance to modern Wiccans and pagans, has been largely discredited among academic historians, and any claims the witchcraft of the period of the witch-hunts might have to the status of an organised and structured religion remain completely unsubstantiated.

A much more hopeful approach to the history of witchcraft 'from below' was established by two British historians, Alan Macfarlane and Keith Thomas, in the early 1970s [94, 102]. Macfarlane was the author of an important book on witchcraft in Essex, his work being distinguished by an exhaustive and imaginative use of court archives and the application of insights derived from twentieth-century social anthropology to early modern witchcraft accusations. Macfarlane's regional study, like Thomas's more general work, demonstrated that in England witchcraft accusations were not generally set in motion by judges or clergymen, but were rather the result of interpersonal tensions between villagers. These tensions, on this model often brought to a head by the refusal of charity demanded by the supposed witch, were the outcome of broader socio-economic changes. Under the pressure of population increase, splits between poorer and richer villagers were becoming more marked, not least because the richer ones were adopting a more commercially-oriented ethic which challenged older views of communal solidarity. What might be described as a social history approach to the history of the witch-craze had been constructed, and was lodged in a familiar and well-documented model of socio-economic development.

This model, perhaps most neatly labelled as the Macfarlane–Thomas paradigm, will be discussed at length later in this book. What needs to be emphasised here is the importance of the work of these two historians in creating a major shift in scholarly interpretations of witchcraft as a historical phenomenon. Historians working on witchcraft throughout Europe, as well as on witchcraft in England's North American colonies, began to reinterpret their subject, and scan demonological tracts and court archives anew in search of evidence of the popular pressures behind witch-hunting. And, of course, such evidence was found to be widespread, which challenged Macfarlane and Thomas's assumption that witch persecution in England was unique, but enriched our understanding of the phenomenon in many other areas. Moreover, historians also began to investigate that other important phenomenon whose importance had been clearly recognised for the first time by Macfarlane and Thomas, the existence of practitioners of 'good' witchcraft, known in England most frequently as cunning (that is, skilled or knowledgeable) men or women. These cunning folk were important in the popular beliefs of the period, and, indeed, it is possible in many areas to find as much evidence of their activities as those of the bad witches who allegedly used occult means to harm or kill humans or their farm animals, to raise storms or to blight the crops.

Another major area of interest among recent historians of witchcraft is the connections between witchcraft and gender, or, more specifically, the reason why something like 80 per cent of those accused and executed for witchcraft during the European witch-craze were women. The question had not been much considered by earlier historians of witchcraft, but it entered the agenda very strongly in the mid-1970s. The crucial development here was the rise of the Women's Movement in the United States and Europe. Women were now consciously involved in a struggle to improve their political, economic and social position and sought to construct a history of oppression which would help inform their consciousness in their ongoing struggle. The women accused and burnt as witches seemed to provide powerful evidence for man's inhumanity to woman: thus we find the authors of one work describing the witch-hunts as 'a ruling class campaign of terror against the female peasant population' [58 p. 6], and the author of another to describe the hunts as a 'specifically Western and Christian manipulation of the androtic state of atrocity', which was 'closely intertwined with phallocentric obsessions with purity' [138 pp. 179, 190].

It should be noted that the authors making such claims rarely had much by way of a track record as researchers into the history of witchcraft, while their insistence on the witch-craze as the outcome of oppression and bigotry made them, ironically, among the last proponents of the Enlightenment, rationalist view of the hunts. Yet there is no denying that they focused attention on an issue of vital importance which had previously been neglected. Although its exact significance remains unresolved, few of those now researching into the history of witchcraft would deny the importance of the gender element, although, equally, few serious historians would now see the problem in terms of a simplistic emphasis upon the male oppression of women. Rather more sophisticated approaches have been opened up by the realisation that not only most of the witches, but also a high proportion of those accusing them or giving evidence against them, were also women. On a popular level, witchcraft, for reasons which we shall explore later, was frequently seen as something which operated within the female social and cultural spheres, or, at least, as a specifically female form of power. But this contention must, of course, recognise the fact that even in the areas where the proportion of those accused of witchcraft was high, there were always a few male witches, while in some parts of Europe a substantial minority, on occasions even a majority, of those accused as witches might be men.

Witchcraft in England: some preliminary comments

So far we have ranged widely, touching on issues which are relevant to the history of witchcraft throughout Europe and Europe's American colonies. Let us, in the closing paragraphs of this introduction, concentrate on the history of witchcraft in England. As we have noted, a paradigm constructed by Alan Macfarlane and Keith Thomas remained the dominant one in English witchcraft studies from the early 1970s until the closing years of the twentieth century. It should be remembered, however, that a number of earlier historians had worked on witchcraft in England, and that their contributions should not be totally forgotten. In 1911 a young American scholar, Wallace Notestein, who was later to gain recognition as a distinguished historian of early Stuart parliaments, published his PhD thesis, an important study which was based primarily on English printed works dating from the period of the witch-trials [95]. In 1929 another American, G.L. Kittredge, published a study of witchcraft in England and New England. This book demonstrated a formidable knowledge of printed sources, and also prefigured some of those assumptions about English witchcraft which were to become central to the Macfarlane–Thomas paradigm [90]. And, if Notestein and Kittredge mastered the printed sources, significant pioneering work on the archival ones was carried out by an Englishman, C. L'Estrange Ewen, who published important books on English witchcraft in 1929 and 1933. Neglected during his lifetime, Ewen's researches are now regarded as pathbreaking [81, 82].

Witchcraft as an object of serious investigation among English historians remained neglected for nearly 40 years after Kittredge and Ewen published their works. Indeed, in 1969, Hugh Trevor-Roper, in the introduction to his study which popularised the concept of the European witch-craze, summed up the position of witchcraft studies in the English-speaking world when he felt it necessary to rebut the opinion that 'the witch-craze is a disgusting subject, below the dignity of history'. As Trevor-Roper commented: 'Disgusting or not, it is also a historical fact, of European significance, and its rise precisely in the years of the Renaissance and Reformation is a problem which must be faced by anyone who is tempted to over-emphasize the "modernity" of that period' [75 *pp. 7, 8*]. A few years later, of course, Macfarlane and Thomas's work demonstrated that, albeit from a very different perspective from that adopted by Trevor-Roper, witchcraft is an important and academically demanding subject which is fully worthy of serious historical analysis. Unfortunately, so fundamental was the contribution of these two scholars that the generality of historians of early modern England felt that the subject had been so well dealt with as to be closed, and continued their investigations into more familiar historical subject areas.

The revival of interest in witchcraft in early modern England which set in from the mid-1990s forms the intellectual backdrop to this book. Two major areas of our current rethinking need in particular to be addressed here. The first is to challenge the notion, central to the Macfarlane–Thomas paradigm but also present in the writings of Notestein, Kittredge and Ewen, that English witchcraft and witch accusations were somehow distinctive from the 'continental' equivalents of these phenomena. English trials were free of some of the more bizarre elements which are to be found in witch-trials in some parts of continental Europe: there is little by way of the sabbat, of night-flying, or of sexual intercourse with incubi or succubi, while even the idea of sexual intercourse between witch and devil came relatively late and uncertainly to England. The English also experienced little by way of officially-directed mass trials of witches. But it is now clear that the English experience of witchcraft and witch-hunting was not unique, but rather that it was a variation on a number of themes which can be found throughout Europe [51, 52]. English demonological writers were familiar with the works of continental demon-ologists, while continental peasants seem to have shared the same con-cerns over *maleficium*, the harm caused by witchcraft, and seem to have much the same sort of recourse to 'good' witches, as did Essex villagers. The German mass-trials of the early seventeenth century, regarded as typical of the 'continental' situation by so many historians of English witchcraft, were in fact atypical of much of continental Europe, and, indeed, of many territories within the Holy Roman Empire. The 'English' pattern of a low intensity of witch-trials, of isolated accusations against the individual witch or small batches of three or four suspects, was to be found in many other European regions. On reflection, the notion that there was a monolithic 'continental' attitude to witchcraft stretching from the Channel coast to the Urals is an inherently improbable one.

The second point arises from Macfarlane and Thomas's major achieve-ment in providing an approach to witchcraft which concentrated on ideas about witchcraft on a popular level, and concentrated on the connections between witchcraft accusations and socio-economic change. Despite its undoubted importance, this approach had the effect of marginalising witchcraft as an intellectual, theological, or indeed political issue. Attention is now being refocused on the intellectual and theological aspects of early modern English witchcraft, while its political aspects are also being reconsidered. The possible political connections, as far as England was concerned, were signalled in a now largely forgotten book, dating from 1947, written by R. Trevor Davies, which attempted, *inter alia*, to establish concern over witchcraft as a central characteristic of the 'Puritan' opponents of Charles I [104]. Davies, like so many writers on witchcraft history, pushed an interesting idea too far: yet it is significant that one of the strands in the most recent writing on witchcraft in early modern England addresses its status as a 'political' issue [e.g., 76].

In this book I shall be developing and elaborating upon the themes raised in this introduction. My main aims will be, firstly, to expand on some of the major interpretations of the subject and, secondly, through the provision of a selection of primary source materials, provide the reader with the opportunity of entering the mental world of people for whom witchcraft was a reality, or at least a live issue. As in any exercise of this sort, constraints of space have meant that enormous areas of documentation have perforce been excluded. Over a hundred books, tracts, and pamphlets on witchcraft were published in England between 1566 and 1736, there are numerous references to witchcraft in the court records of the period, while it is also mentioned in contemporary theological works of a more general nature, and in diaries and letters. Using such sources, I hope to leave the reader with the impression that witchcraft is a more complex, demanding and serious historical phenomenon than might at first have been supposed. I also hope, in the process, to convince the reader that the subject is a fascinating one.

2

Elite perspectives on witchcraft: demonology, the law and educated culture

If beliefs in witchcraft, or something very like it, have been found in most known societies, they have certainly been present in Europe since antiquity. What was different in Europe between the mid-fifteenth and the mid-eighteenth centuries was that the witch was regarded not as an isolated magical practitioner, but rather as a member of an anti-Christian sect, a being eager to overturn the moral and physical universe of God, Christian believer, and Christian ruler alike. Something of the flavour of this conception of the witch was conveyed by the great English theologian William Perkins (1558–1602), glossing the frequently discussed biblical text I Samuel XV.23, 'For rebellion is as the sin of witchcraft':

> It is a principle of the law of nature, holden for a grounded truth in all countries & kingdomes, among all people in every age; that the traytor, who is an enemie to the state, and rebelleth against his lawfull prince, should be put to death; now the most notorious traytor and rebell that can be, is the witch. For shee renounceth God himselfe, the king of kings, shee leaves the societie of his church and people, shee bindeth herself in league with the devill. [36 *pp. 248–9*]

It was this ability on the part of contemporaries to see the witch as a general enemy, as the foe both of the king's laws and those of God, which allows us to talk of 'witch-hunts' or of the 'European witch-craze'.

The law and witchcraft

In England, witchcraft and witch-trials prior to the mid-sixteenth century remain obscure and ill-documented subjects. Most English monarchs from Richard II onwards, like their counterparts in other European states, found themselves confronted by what might be termed treason-cum-sorcery plots [123], in which those planning the downfall of the monarch sought magical assistance (suspicions of witchcraft, to take a familiar example, were present during the trial of Anne Boleyn in 1536). On a less exalted social level, occasional references to witches can be found in both ecclesiast-ical and secular court records. These involved accusations against harmful witches and cunning folk, while it seems that many of the practices associated with witches in the Elizabethan and Stuart periods were already the subject of popular belief by the early sixteenth century, and probably much earlier. But the number of such cases was few, and the English ecclesiastical authorities do not seem to have seen witchcraft as a major problem. Our current state of knowledge suggests that there was no English contribution to the formation of demonological theory, while insofar as witchcraft figured in pre-Reformation tracts it was recourse to cunning folk, rather than the threat posed by harmful witches, which seems to have been seen as the most consistent cause for concern.

Legally, despite the occasional trial of witchcraft in the secular courts, witchcraft was not defined as a crime under the law of England until 1542, with the statute 33 Hen. VIII, cap. 8. There is no evidence that this, the most harsh of English witchcraft statutes, was ever enforced, and it was in any case repealed along with other criminal legislation of Henry VIII's reign in 1547 (statute 1 Edw. VI, cap. 12). The important Act came in 1563, with statute 5 Eliz. I, cap. 12, which re-established witch-craft as a felony [*Doc. 1*]. Under this legislation, killing people by witch-craft was punishable by death. Injuring people or animals or damaging goods by witchcraft, attempting to do the same, using witchcraft to find lost or stolen goods, money, or treasure, or using witchcraft to provoke love or for any other purpose, were punishable by a year's imprisonment punctuated by four spells on the pillory for the first offence, and death on the second. A further Act of 1604 (1 Jac. I, cap. 12) made injuring people a capital offence on the first conviction, reasserted the 1563 statute's clause making the conjuration of spirits a capital offence, and added and made capital the curious offence of using dead bodies, or parts of them, for witchcraft or sorcery.

Traditionally, the Elizabethan statute was interpreted as being connected with the establishment of a new Protestant regime after the accession of Elizabeth I in 1558, while, more specifically, it has been suggested that there was a decisive input by returned Marian exiles who had added a desire to hunt witches to the other aspects of advanced Protestantism which they had picked up during their continental sojourn. This last connection has always defied solid proof, and the most recent research has revealed a somewhat more complex situation [122]. It appears that the 1563 witchcraft Act, along with an Act against false prophesying (5 Eliz. I, cap. 15) was passed because a group of Catholic plotters were discovered, in yet another episode of treason-cum-sorcery, using sorcery and witchcraft against Elizabeth's regime, and that the authorities were dismayed to discover that there was no law in existence to try them under for this particular aspect of their activities. It should be noted that although Catholicism was never fully equated with witchcraft, for the English Protestant theologian of the time the two were in many ways closely associated: at the very least, both were seen as dangerous and possibly destructive superstitions. In the aftermath of the trial and conviction of the Catholic plotters, the Privy Council seems to have pushed for new laws against Catholics, sorcerers, witches, and false prophesies. The details of how the Act progressed through parliament need not detain us here, although it should be noted that the bishops appear to have taken a keen interest in it. What is obvious is that the 1563 Act was the product of a distinct historical conjuncture, although it is certain that the Elizabethan regime, like any responsible European government of the period, would have enacted legislation against witches at an early point. 1563 was, for example, also the year in which another recently established and worried Protestant regime, that existing in Scotland, passed a witchcraft Act.

Demonology

It is noteworthy that witchcraft appeared as a crime on the English statute book, and as a crime prosecuted in the secular courts, before

English theologians had constructed a comprehensive model of satanic witchcraft: indeed, it is one of the peculiarities of English witchcraft history that the first major book on witchcraft published by an English-man, Reginald Scot's *Discoverie of Witchcraft* of 1584, was an unrelent-ingly sceptical work written by an obscure country gentleman. There was, however, a flurry of demonological writing in England in the late Elizabethan and Jacobean periods. The first such work, *A Treatise against Witchcraft*, was published by a Cambridge-educated clergyman and theo-logian, Henry Holland, in 1590. In 1608 there came a more significant book, William Perkins' *Discourse of the Damned Art of Witchcraft*. Perkins was the leading English theologian of his day, and his work on witch-craft, published posthumously, was to prove influential in debates about witchcraft in England throughout the seventeenth century. Other demono-logical works were published by an obscure clergyman Alexander Roberts, in 1616 [39] and the rather better known Thomas Cooper in 1617 [10], while in 1616 (there was a second edition in 1625 [11]) the Cambridge-trained physician John Cotta published a tract on the med-ical aspects of witchcraft. In 1627 came the last work in this series, Richard Bernard's *A Guide to Grand Iury Men*. Bernard (1568–1641) was an important clerical writer, and his short work, reprinted in 1629, was in many ways a summing-up of what was arguably a distinctive style of English demonological writing.

If a distinctive English demonological style emerged, it should be remembered that the broad theological framework within which it oper-ated was one which was shared, albeit with different emphases, by all European demonological writers of the period. For witchcraft to oper-ate, three elements were needed: divine permission, satanic power and malevolence, and human agency in the shape of the witch. The role allocated to divine power was of central importance. It was unthinkable that the devil could be as powerful as God, a position (known technically as Dualism) which was in any case heretical. Demonological writers had, therefore, to square the circle of warning their readers of the dreadful-ness of Satan's powers and Satan's snares, yet of assuring them that he could not, in the last resort, overcome God and his people. The demono-logists then had the problem of explaining why God allowed witchcraft to happen at all, an interesting facet of the broader question of how

Christian theologians accounted for the presence of evil in the world. Their standard explanations revolved around the argument that witchcraft was one of the means which God used to chasten sinful humankind in general, to punish individual sinners, to shake up the godly who might be sliding into sinfulness, and to test the faith of the individual believer. It is no accident that the Book of Job figures frequently in English Protestant theologians' writings on explaining how the good Christian should react to witchcraft both psychologically and practically.

There were numerous other themes which surface regularly in English demonological tracts: the power of the Devil, the extent of his ability to affect the workings of nature, the need to assure readers that the occult powers at the disposal of the Devil and witches could only create *mira*, or illusions, rather than real miracles, *miracula*. In common with Protestant writers abroad, English demonologists placed little emphasis on the witches' sabbat, where witches supposedly met for cannibalistic feasts and orgiastic group sex, or about the related issue of night-flying, or about sexual intercourse between human beings and demons. They did, however, afford a central importance to the demonic pact, the bargain by which the witch renounced God her maker, and gave her soul to the devil in return for the ability to do harm [*Doc. 2*]. There was, unfortunately, no direct scriptural basis for the existence of the pact, a matter of some consequence to writers who saw scripture as their main source of authority. But Protestant logic helped here: the pact with the devil was the inversion of the covenant between the Almighty and the Christian believer. As Thomas Cooper put it, 'as God has a covenant with man: so will Satan have a special covenant also with his servants' [10 *p. 30*].

There was another emphasis in English, and perhaps more generally Protestant, demonological writing. For most of the authors we are considering here (notably Holland, Perkins, Cooper, Bernard and another writer whom we shall encounter shortly, George Gifford), the works they wrote on witchcraft were only one aspect of their literary output, one aspect of a broader body of theological, evangelical and pastoral writing. The underlying thrust of this writing was the problem of how to bring the English to a proper understanding of correct Christian belief and conduct, and thus lead them to the setting up of a godly commonwealth where human beings could be recreated in a new, more godly, mould.

Extirpating malefic witchcraft was only one aspect of this process, and was far from the most important one. More significant was the wider need to eradicate beliefs and practices which the English Protestant mind defined as 'superstition'. An obvious target here were the rituals of the Roman Catholic church, but for our writers the concept of 'superstition' extended to a host of popular beliefs and customs. Perhaps the most avidly attacked of these, in the context of writings on witchcraft, was resorting to good witches, cunning folk. These, to English demonological writers, were considered as even more harmful than malefic witches [*Doc. 3*]. Like the malefic witches, the 'good' witches surely derived their powers from the devil, but were even more harmful than malefic witches in that they drew the populace away from right religion, and pretended to do good when they in fact did evil. English Protestant demonological writers seem to have devoted as much space in their tracts to excoriating the 'good' witch as they did to expressing their horror of the activities of the bad ones.

But, ironically, the attack on 'superstition', carried to what at least some contemporaries regarded as its logical conclusion, potentially fostered an extremely sceptical position on the power of witches and witchcraft. Most Protestant writers stressed the importance of divine providence, of the universal intervention of God into human affairs, and some were anxious to bring their readers to a realisation that most of the misfortunes they attributed to witches were, in fact, attributable to God. Even demonologists like Perkins were acutely aware of this issue, and in the hands of writers who afforded a central importance to divine providence the concept could be extended to create an almost complete marginalisation of malefic witchcraft as it was understood by the bulk of the population. Thus it might be, and frequently was, argued that an over-anxious belief in witches could overestimate the power of both the Devil and his human agents. It is vital to grasp that there was no single, hegemonic theological line on witchcraft [*Doc. 4*]. It was possible for perfectly orthodox Protestants like Henry Holland or William Perkins to argue that witchcraft was a real threat, an aspect of Satan's struggle against God and his people, and for other perfectly orthodox Protestants to argue that witchcraft was a phenomenon whose significance, as it was conceived by most of their less well-informed contemporaries, was misconceived and largely illusory. This argument was stated with clarity and force by Reginald Scot, and was present in the writings of the Puritan minister George Gifford, author of a number of religious tracts, and a keen observer of witchcraft beliefs around his living at Maldon in south Essex [22, 119, 125].

Thus by the time Richard Bernard published his *Guide to Grand Iury Men* in 1627 there was a sizeable, complex, and theoretically sophisticated body of demonological writing in existence in England. But even in an age which took theology seriously, much of this demonological writing was a little abstruse for the less-educated reader. However, for nearly a quarter of a century before Henry Holland published the first major English work against witchcraft, the English reading public had been regaled with accounts of witchcraft and witch-trials contained in tracts and pamphlets aimed at a broad audience [87, 99]. The first of these came in 1566, when one tract described the trial of three malefic witches in Essex, another the investigation by the ecclesiastical authorities of a sorcerer named John Walsh at Exeter [17, 18]. These were followed by descriptions of trials in Berkshire and Essex in 1579, in Essex again in 1582 [38, 16, 44], and of the celebrated case of the Witches of Warboys in 1593 [34]. There were a number of subsequent pamphlets, among them a notable account of the trial in 1612 of the Pendle Hill witches at Lancaster [37], and the series effectively ended in 1621 with the description of the trial and execution of a woman named Elizabeth Sawyer from Edmonton in Middlesex [24]. This last was written by Henry Goodcole, a London clergyman who ministered to the prisoners in Newgate gaol, and who was author of a number of tracts describing notorious crimes and setting them in an appropriate moral framework. His pamphlet on the Sawyer case included the confession he had elicited from the condemned witch while preparing her spiritually for execution.

These tracts and pamphlets varied in length: the ones describing the Essex case of 1582 and the witches of Warboys ran to about 100 pages, while the tract describing the trial of the Lancashire witches in 1612 was also lengthy; others amounted to only a few pages, and some later examples were simply single-page broadsheets. They also varied in tone, some being more overtly sensational than others. But most of them, as well as describing the events constituting their core subject matter, contained passages (often in the form of a foreword or epistle to the reader) which pointed out the moral of the story the tract was telling, placing it firmly in the broader context of the cosmic struggle between good and evil which underlay most educated thinking on witchcraft. Even these supposedly 'popular' tracts conveyed a clear and theologically informed view of witchcraft, and a clear warning of the dangers of Satan's snares. We know little about the readership of these tracts, or of their impact, but their general significance must have been to reinforce the view of witches as the devil's agents, in league with their master in the great work of undermining the laws of God and man. This propaganda element was perhaps most obvious in the tract published in 1613 which described, at considerable length, the Lancashire trials of the previous year. It author was Thomas Potts, the clerk of the assizes which tried the witches, and it was apparently composed at the direction of the presiding judges, Sir James Altham and Sir Edward Bromley, who felt the matters revealed during the trials so remarkable that 'we thought it necessarie to publish them to the world'. At the end of the tract Potts prayed 'God graunt us the long and prosperous continuance of these honorable and reverend judges, under whose government we live in these North parts: for we may say, that God Almightie hath singled them out, and set them on his seat, for the defence of Justice'. The Pendle witches, hanged ostensibly for the harm they had done their neighbours, had been defeated by the agents of the godly commonwealth, a 'great deliverance' which had defeated a challenge to both secular and divine order [37 *sig. Z3*].

Witchcraft, magic and educated culture

The tendency to regard official attitudes to witchcraft mainly as a religious affair, and for recent historians of the topic to concentrate on witchcraft as something essentially of concern to peasants, has tended to obscure the importance of magic and the occult in educated culture [73]. The neoplatonism which became fashionable as the sixteenth century progressed encouraged this, and what modern categorisation would describe as science or medicine remained inseparable from magic. This confusion is, for England, perhaps best summed up in the person of John Dee

(1527–1608) [77, 83]. Born in London, Dee was educated at Cambridge, but in 1547 went to the Low Countries to extend his intellectual contacts, progressing from there to France, where he was offered the post of professor of mathematics at the university of Paris. He returned to England, survived Mary Tudor's reign, and after the accession of Elizabeth I in 1558 more or less established himself as the new queen's court astrologer, one of his first tasks in this capacity being to cast a horoscope to help establish the best date for her coronation. He went abroad in 1584, among other places visiting Prague, then a hotbed of occult learning, and became increasingly interested in alchemy and in attempting to raise angels, this latter activity being aided by ever more elaborate mathematical calculations. Needless to say, Dee occasionally fell foul of accusations of sorcery, and in 1580 a mob, thinking him to be a witch, ransacked his house at Mortlake and destroyed or carried off his scientific instruments and equipment.

Few could aspire to being the sort of Renaissance magus of European standing that John Dee was. But throughout the sixteenth and seventeenth centuries there was widespread dabbling among the educated and well-born in alchemy, the attempt to turn base metals into gold by occult means, while belief in astrology was widespread, and many of its practitioners regarded it as an exact science. The mid-seventeenth century was to witness the career of William Lilly, an astrologer whose clientele included lowly seekers after information and advice on the one hand, and, on the other, the 1640s parliamentarian regime who felt moved to seek astrological predictions about its military endeavours [96]. Lilly was by no means an isolated figure. Doctors, from leading London physicians to the better-educated cunning folk, would use horoscopes to aid their diagnosis and treatment, while, certainly in 1600, most doctors were happy to use charms as a means to aid recovery and ward off sickness [92]. Hard-line Protestant theologians railed against such practices, and were especially hostile to astrology: the practices continued, nevertheless, to enjoy widespread acceptance. The relationship between educated views on magic and the occult and popular beliefs about witchcraft remain problematic, but it does seem safe to assert that the widespread acceptance of the reality of magical and occult influences at an elite level helped convince the educated that malefic witchcraft existed.

Classical culture constituted another factor reinforcing the acceptance of witchcraft and related phenomena among the educated. In the sixteenth and seventeenth centuries education, certainly for those not destined to become clergymen, was largely restricted to training in Latin and Greek and immersion in classical texts. And, of course, classical texts contained some very overt references to witchcraft and magic. The works of continental demonologists were scattered with such references, and English demonologists (although generally preferring to draw on scripture as an authority) made use of them. They were familiar to educated gentry. The Yorkshire gentleman Edward Fairfax, for example, drew on references from Virgil, Horace, and Theocritus when the supposed bewitchment of his daughters early in the 1620s focused his attention on the problem of witchcraft, although it should be noted that Fairfax already had a reputation as a translator of Latin verse into English [12 pp. 74–5]. Above all, the dramatists of the Elizabethan and Jacobean period, anxious to display their learning to their audiences and patrons, made heavy use of them. To take the best-known example, the witch scenes in Shakespeare's *Macbeth*, probably first staged in 1606, made as much use of classical models as they did of contemporary witch beliefs. Witchcraft was firmly located in the ancient world in John Marston's *The Wonder of Women or the Tragedy of Sophonisba* published in the same year, while the antimasque to Ben Jonson's *Masque of Queens*, performed before the royal court in 1609, was suffused with classical allusions [*Doc. 5*].

Prosecution at the courts

These broader cultural and intellectual currents, although doubtlessly present in the minds of judges, justices of the peace, the petty gentlemen who sat on grand juries and screened formal accusations of witchcraft, and the writers who composed the pamphlets describing witch-trials, receive scant mention in the formal legal records of the period. A number of courts could try witchcraft. The ecclesiastical courts still investigated sorcery, and many fortune tellers and cunning folk were presented before them, usually receiving an admonition or a light punishment. In secular courts, the crime of witchcraft, as defined by the statutes of 1563 and 1604, could be tried at quarter sessions, courts held four times annually for each of England's counties and presided over by justices of the peace, local gentry frequently with little or no legal training, while accusations of witchcraft might also be tried at local borough courts, many of which had the rights of gaol delivery, and hence the ability to try felony, including witchcraft. At the borough courts, too, the legal expertise of those running the courts might be of a variable quality. For the most part, however, in England cases of malefic witchcraft were tried at the assizes [81].

The assizes, whose origins lay in the twelfth century, constituted a neat and generally effective method of bringing centrally directed justice to the localities. For the purposes of the assizes, England's counties were grouped into six circuits, and twice a year, in January and around Midsummer, two judges were allocated to each of these assize circuits, and sent out from Westminster to try criminal cases in the provinces. The English criminal law differed from the Roman Law systems operating in most territories in western and central Europe, most obviously in the way in which it depended upon juries to establish proof, and did not employ torture as a normal part of criminal trial process. But, so far as the history of witchcraft is concerned, perhaps the crucial difference between the English criminal trial and its equivalent in many other states lay in the quality of the judges. Over much of continental Europe the decision to execute witches was made in local, sometimes even village, courts run by amateur judges with little or no legal training. In England, trials were presided over by experienced and senior judges who were culturally distanced from the world of village squabbles that so often formed the context of witchcraft accusations. This distancing process was enhanced by a convention, only occasionally ignored, that assize judges could not ride the circuit wherein lay the county in which their main residence was located.

Sadly, most assize records for the relevant period have been lost: the only circuit for which indictments against witches, the formal charges on which they stood trial, survive in bulk is the South-Eastern or Home Circuit, comprising the counties of Essex, Hertfordshire, Kent, Surrey and Sussex. Even here the survival of indictments is not complete: about a quarter of assize files for the Elizabethan and Stuart periods are missing, and there is no way of telling how many witchcraft indictments these may have contained. Those that do survive, however, present a clear impression of the ebb and flow of criminal charges of witchcraft [81, 100 *pp. 105–14*]. Such charges rose steadily in number from the 1560s, peaked at a total of more than 180 in the 1580s, stayed high in the 1590s, and then fell away precipitously in the early seventeenth century, with less than twenty indictments in the 1630s. There was a small peak in the 1640s and 1650s, with maybe 130 indictments in the two decades combined, this being largely attributable to a group of indictments associated with the Matthew Hopkins trials in Essex in 1645, and with several local panics in Kent. After 1660, indictments returned to their 1620s level, the last known trial on this circuit, involving a Hertfordshire woman named Jane Wenham, coming in 1712 [9, 20, 117]. Within the five counties, indictments for witchcraft were at their highest in Essex, which engendered 464 indictments, well over half the total for the circuit as a whole. At the other end of the scale, Sussex experienced 36 indictments and one execution, a figure which makes the concept of a 'European witch-craze' seem a trifle hyperbolic.

Although evidence upon which similar calculations might be based simply does not survive from the other assize circuits, there are further bodies of court materials which help challenge the Home Circuit model. Middlesex, a heavily populated county which abutted both London and several of the counties in the Home Circuit, enjoyed an independent jurisdiction over felony. There were at least 63 indictments for witchcraft involving 40 people tried before the Middlesex sessions [82 *pp. 430–5*] (to put witch-trials into perspective, it should be noted that between 1550 and 1625 alone a total of some 7,660 indictments for felonies of all types survive from this county [148 *p. 80*]). Peak periods of prosecution here were in 1610–19, and 1650–59. Cheshire in the north-west, a palatinate county, also had a peculiar jurisdiction over felony, serious crime in the county usually being tried before the Court of Great Sessions at Chester, which enjoyed what were essentially the same powers as the assizes. A trickle of cases of witchcraft and sorcery were tried by the Court of Great Sessions. The first involving malefic witchcraft came in 1590, when a woman was accused of bewitching a cow, the first involving a human victim coming in 1613. Altogether 69 indictments for witchcraft and sorcery were brought before the Court of Great Sessions, the last of these being in 1675, with something of a peak in the 1650s, a decade which experienced 22 indictments, with a total of seven people, all of them women, sentenced to death [82 *pp. 413–22*].

Three points emerge from these samples of court statistics. Firstly, with the exception perhaps of Essex in the last two decades of the sixteenth century, witchcraft indictments formed only a tiny fraction of the courts' criminal business. Secondly, acquittal rates were high. To take the largest sample, on the Home Circuit of the assizes only 104, or 22 per cent, of the 474 accused of witchcraft were sentenced to death. In Middlesex a quarter of those accused were convicted, not all of them capitally, while in Cheshire, as we have seen, 69 indictments generated only seven death sentences. And, in all three samples, the overwhelming majority of those accused of malefic witchcraft were women: over 90 per cent on the Home Circuit, 87.5 per cent in Middlesex.

As we have noted, church courts also enjoyed jurisdiction over alleged witches and sorcerers. An extensive ecclesiastical court system had survived the Reformation, and from the middle of Elizabeth's reign the church courts were employed more and more actively to discipline the public into habits of regular church attendance and correct moral behaviour. Although the 1563 statute had taken malefic witchcraft out of the church courts' control, they still tried sorcerers, cunning folk and fortune tellers, local dabblers in what were often very folklorised versions of the occult. Typical presentments before the church courts might include being a cunning man or woman or resorting to such people, instances where the person presented was simply described as a witch or, in some ways most intriguing of all, cases when people with a reputation for being a witch tried to turn the tables on those thus describing them by suing them for defamation. So far few exhaustive analyses of ecclesiastical court records have been carried out, especially for the post-1660 period, and such analyses as have been completed present a contradictory picture. Essex, in what may have been yet another of that county's peculiarities as far as witchcraft was concerned, experienced numerous presentments involving witchcraft and sorcery before the county's archdeaconry courts, with minor peaks in 1566 and 1605 and a larger one, involving twenty presentments, in 1589. After 1620, however, prosecutions at the ecclesiastical courts in Essex seem to have ended [94 *p. 70*]. In Yorkshire 177 presentments were recorded in the archbishop's visitation records between 1567 and 1640, hardly a massive total for England's largest county [136]. In Wiltshire, presentments for witchcraft before the church courts over the same sort of period were almost unknown [142 *pp. 97, 113–14*].

A decline in official concern?

Such evidence as we have, indeed, suggests that by the 1630s the prosecution of witchcraft was becoming very rare. The Home Circuit indictments, the records of the Middlesex Sessions, the archives of the church courts on Essex and Yorkshire: all of these demonstrate that accusations of witchcraft and sorcery came before the courts only very infrequently after Charles I came to the throne in 1625. And in 1633–34 there came an incident which suggests strongly that central government was becoming very hostile to witch-hunting. In 1633 an eleven-year-old boy named Edmund Robinson, living near Pendle in Lancashire, became the centre of what might have been a very severe witch-panic after claiming to have been taken to the sabbat by a witch, and to have seen a number of local women there whom he identified as witches. Frustratingly, surviving records are too fragmentary to permit a full reconstruction of this incident, but its outlines are clear [100 *pp. 126–7*]. The judge who tried the first few cases to emerge from Robinson's statements became alarmed when he realised that accusations were mounting quickly, and invoked the aid of central government. The bishop of Chester was instructed to investigate the matter, and soon after Robinson, his father, and a few of the suspects were taken down to London. There the boy and his father were questioned, while the suspected witches were made the subjects of a medical investigation carried out by a team headed by that most eminent of doctors, William Harvey. Harvey and his assistants could find little by way of witches' marks on the suspected women, while Robinson confessed that he had confected the tale of being taken to the sabbat as an excuse for being late getting the cattle home. What is striking is how the central authorities, alerted by a worried judge, acted quickly and decisively to prevent what could have been an outbreak of witch-hunting far larger than the celebrated 1612 Lancashire trials.

Concern about witchcraft at the centre of government had been waning for some time. James I, whatever his reputation as a witch-hunter in Scotland, as king of England displayed his knowledge of witchcraft through exposing fraudulent accusations rather than discovering nests of malefic witches [124]. Moreover, whatever the beliefs of clerical demonologists like Perkins, Cooper or Bernard, the top echelons of the hierarchy of the Church of England had long since shown themselves sceptical. The key issues here were demonic possession and exorcism [93, 101, 105]. The Church of England, in common with other Protestant churches, defied the efficacy of the Catholic rite of exorcism, recommending prayer and fasting as the means of coping with possession. This meant, of course, that the Catholics could use successful exorcisms as propaganda, and the church authorities became very worried about a series of exorcisms carried out in 1585–86, under the direction of a Jesuit priest named William Weston, which were reputed to have attracted several thousand converts to Rome. But the church authorities also faced problems in this respect from extreme Protestants, and concern about over-enthusiastic dispossessions became a facet of the anti-Puritanism which set in at the top of the Church of England in the closing years of Elizabeth's reign. The key figure here was John Darrell, an obscure preacher who carried out a number of dispossessions (usually connected with accusations of witchcraft) in the north and the midlands. Darrell's luck ran out in 1599, when he was involved in the case of a supposedly possessed youth named William Somers at Nottingham [98]. The local authorities became disturbed by the large crowds coming to see the possessed young man, the affair seems to have stirred up religious factionalism in the town, while there was danger of a local witch-panic, with Somers accusing a number of women of sending demons into his body. Darrell was entrusted to the care of the bishop of London, Richard Bancroft, who exposed his activities with Somers as fraudulent, and had his chaplain, Samuel Harsnett, write a propaganda tract to that effect (Darrell and his associates published a number of works in his defence [26, 13]).

No sooner had the Darrell affair ended, than Bancroft was faced by an instance of witchcraft and possession in his own diocese, involving the alleged bewitchment of a fourteen-year-old girl named Mary Glover in

1602 [93]. Although the supposed witch in this case was convicted, Bancroft tried to orchestrate the woman's defence, being especially active in trying to mobilise medical evidence on her behalf, and also waged a campaign against the Puritan clergymen who had supported the accusation and who had been involved in Mary Glover's dispossession. Then in 1605 there came the case of Anne Gunter, a girl of about twenty who was allegedly bewitched and possessed, and whose father had taken her to meet that royal demonologist, James I [101]. James had promptly handed the girl over to Bancroft, by now Archbishop of Canterbury, who delegated the investigation of her case to Harsnett. The girl was soon confessing that she had simulated being possessed at her father's instigation, and father and daughter were duly tried at Star Chamber for false accusations of witchcraft against three women from their home village. This prosecution was almost certainly directed by Bancroft, while in 1603 his propagandist Harsnett had published his *Declaration of egregious popish Impostures*. This work revived memories of the 1580s exorcisms, and was aimed to discredit the Jesuits who were then involved in disputes with more conservative English Catholics. But in this book, which was officially sanctioned, Harsnett came very near to denying the existence of witchcraft, at least as the phenomenon was understood by most of his compatriots. After the accession of Charles, the religious mode represented by Bancroft and Harsnett became dominant. A more relaxed type of Protestantism, frequently described as Arminianism, became fashionable, and this religious style was less amenable to witch-hunting than the harder line, covenant-based Puritanism of William Perkins. Richard Neile, Archbishop of York from 1631, had, as a young man of promise, been involved in the investigation of Anne Gunter and the subsequent Star Chamber proceedings against her and her father. He was also later to be a patron of that great architect of Arminianism and clerical supporter of Charles I's Personal Rule, William Laud.

The import for the history of witchcraft of this religious shift still remains unexplored: historians of the Personal Rule of Charles have not been much concerned with witchcraft. The one work which investigates the theme, while suggestive, is now rather outdated and in any case overstates its case, although it is perhaps noteworthy that kinsfolk of both Oliver Cromwell and Sir Thomas Fairfax had supposedly suffered from witchcraft [104]. There are, however, occasional shards of evidence supporting the contention that by the 1630s the authorities were becoming very averse to witch-hunting. In July 1636, for example, the assize judges on circuit in Somerset made the following order:

> Whereas Elizabeth Stile, widdowe, was indicted att this assizes for witchcraft and upon her tryall was acquitted, and forasmuch as it appeared to this court that she was maliciously, prosecuted by her adversaries, it is ordered by this court att the humble request of the said Elizabeth that she shalbe admitted *in forma pauperis* to bringe her accion against Nicholas Hobbes and all or any other of her prosecutors. And Mr. Glanvill, Mr. Rolles, Mr. Fynche, and Mr. Morgan are assigned to her councell, and Mr. Morgan to be her attorney therein. [149 *p. 28*]

Too much should not be made of one scrap of evidence, but this entry would seem to be symptomatic of a more general mood of official scepticism about witchcraft accusations. Three of those appointed as Elizabeth Stiles's councellours, John Glanvill, Henry Rolle, and Nathaniel Finch, were eminent junior lawyers with a good career in front of them: the court was obviously allocating first-rate legal assistance to the falsely accused woman.

By the 1630s, then, it would seem that in official circles witchcraft was something of a dead issue. Few cases were coming before the courts, and those that were tried almost invariably led to an acquittal. Trial pamphlets, regularly published in the Elizabethan and Jacobean periods, had ceased to appear after the publication of Henry Goodcole's description of the Elizabeth Sawyer case. Richard Bernard's *Guide to Grand Iury Men* reached a second edition in 1629, but no new demonological works were published in the 1630s. A play was written and staged in the wake of the 1633–34 Lancashire affair [97 *pp. 234–6*], but the vogue for witchcraft which was such a feature of the early Jacobean drama was long over. A number of other European states were similarly showing an increased scepticism about witchcraft by this time. To take the most pertinent example, in France the very senior judges of the Paris *Parlement* were proving as cautious about witchcraft as were their English equivalents at assize trials, and were regularly overturning death sentences against witches which came to them on appeal from provincial courts [74]. There was every indication that by the 1630s in England, as in France, and countries such as Spain and the Dutch Republic where witch-hunting had never taken hold, both lay and clerical authorities were very much marginalising witchcraft, and relegating it to the world of popular beliefs and superstitions. But, as we shall see, fate had some surprises in store for both Charles I and his regime, surprises which were of considerable import for English witchcraft history.

3

Witch-trials, witchcraft accusations and the problem of community

Our examination of what might be termed elite perspectives on witchcraft has, therefore, revealed a complex situation: there were a variety of theological emphases; there was the approach to witchcraft as set out in the law; there were the ways, perhaps most clearly demonstrated in the classical learning and in the drama of the period, in which witchcraft operated in the more general culture; and there was also the relationship, via the pervasive influence of magic and the occult on educated thinking, between witchcraft and medicine and what modern terminology would describe as science. Witchcraft was, however, clearly also a matter of some concern to the bulk of the population who were non-elite, not educated to the best standards of the period, and illiterate or, at best, semi-literate. The beliefs of these people are less well documented than those of their social superiors. We must reconstruct what they thought from scattered shards of evidence rather than from weighty treatises, while most of those shards of evidence which do survive were written by members of the elite who were rarely concerned to record the views of the populace at large comprehensively or in a favourable light. Trial records and other forms of court documentation fall into this category, as do the usually hostile comments on popular superstitions which can be found in both demonological works and in sceptical tracts.

Despite these caveats, the evidence which does survive suggests that witch beliefs among the population at large were as rich and complex as, if in many respects rather different from, those held by the educated. We shall explore this proposition more fully in the next chapter; here we shall concentrate on the evidence about witchcraft created by what was, in effect, a phenomenon which constituted the most important interface between elite and popular beliefs on witchcraft: the witch-trial. Formal trials were, of course, only one of the arenas where witch beliefs operated, but the sources recording and describing these trials do provide modern observers with most of their evidence for reconstructing what the early modern English thought about witchcraft, what sort of harm they thought witches were likely to do to them, and what sorts of tensions between neighbours were likely to result in an accusation of witchcraft. The accusation of witchcraft and the subsequent trial contain that dramatic dynamic which many would see as the essence of the history of witchcraft in the early modern period. For those who regard the phenomenon of the witch persecutions as undilutedly horrific and atrocious, the accusation, trial, and subsequent execution of women and men for perpetrating acts which they and any other human being were incapable of performing necessarily assume centrality. Yet, as we shall see, here as elsewhere with the history of witchcraft, closer investigation provides a rather more complex impression of the processes at play.

Prosecution and the pressure 'from below'

There is a well-established interpretation which portrays witch-hunting and witch-trials essentially as a product of the intolerance and bigotry of the judges who staffed the legal apparatus of the state, and of the clergymen who created the learned demonology which provided the ideological underpinning for the judges' witch-persecuting activities. We must reiterate that what made the witch-craze possible was the emergence of a distinctive Christian notion of the witch as the participator in a Satanic heresy, and it is equally evident that neither the witch-craze nor the individual witch-trial could have occurred without the existence of legal systems which accepted the existence of malefic witchcraft as a crime and which were willing to punish that crime through formal legal process. But it is important to grasp that most of those persons tried for witchcraft in early modern England (and, one suspects, in most other parts of Europe) found themselves in court as a result of actions levelled against them by their neighbours. This was recognised by G.L. Kittredge in his pioneering study of 1929 [90 *p. 3*], and was, of course, absolutely central to the interpretation of English witchcraft put forward by Alan Macfarlane and Keith Thomas in the early 1970s [94, 102]. To understand witchcraft accusations, we must therefore enter the world of popular beliefs, and the narrow universes of the village communities within which witches and their supposed victims, the people who made the witchcraft accusations, lived.

The quality of life in England's village communities remains problematic. Obviously, the sheer number of such communities (there were about 10,000 parishes in England, most of them rural) makes it impossible to be unequivocal on this issue, as does their variety: rural parishes differed in their geographic extent, in the size and density of their populations, and in their economic life. Trying to generalise about the nature of human relationships within such a variety of contexts is clearly difficult. Few historians would now accept the traditional view, fostered as an antidote to nineteenth-century fears over industrialisation and urbanisation, that the pre-industrial village was a stable, harmonious and co-operative environment which allowed its inhabitants to lead lives more happy and fulfilling than those of later industrial workers. The problem is to determine how far to go in a more pessimistic direction which would see the populations of such settlements as atomised and riven by feuds. Keith Thomas, in his discussion of the social background to witchcraft accusations, wrote of a 'tyranny of local opinion' which was frequently crucial in defining individuals as witches [102 *p. 527*]. Pessimism to the extent of caricature on this issue has, to take an important example, been offered by Lawrence Stone:

> Overwhelming evidence of the lack of warmth and tolerance in interpersonal relations at the village level is provided by the extraordinary amount of back-biting, malicious slander, marital discord and unfaithfulness, and petty spying and delation . . . the Elizabethan village was a place filled with malice and hatred, its only unifying bond being the occasional episode of mass hysteria, which temporarily bound together the majority in order to harry and persecute the local witch. [150 *p. 98*]

Other sources have presented a more reassuring impression. Richard Gough, one of the few contemporaries to leave us an impression of his home village (Myddle in Shropshire), had a clear idea of what a decent neighbour was like, and his account of seventeenth-century Myddle shows that most of its inhabitants shared this notion, however imperfectly they may have achieved it [140]. One suspects that the inhabitants of Myddle, and indeed of most other English villages of the period, had rather more than hysteria against the local witch binding them together.

The social and economic structures of these communities, as we have suggested, varied, with the heavily populated and economically advanced villages of south-eastern England and East Anglia demonstrating different characteristics from, say, Lakeland parishes with their scattered settlement patterns and their pastoral farming. Yet throughout England the sixteenth and seventeenth centuries constituted a period of marked, if in most areas gradual, socio-economic change [147 *part 2*]. The key was demographic growth: over the period *c.* 1530–1630 the population of England doubled, from maybe 2,500,000 to 5,000,000 people. Food production barely kept up with this increase, while this demographic growth also created a flooded labour market which meant that the substantial proportion of the population which was wholly or partly dependent on wage labour found it more difficult to get work, and received less in terms of real wages for such employment as they were able to find. The price of bread, the essential food of the poor, was by 1650 at about six times its 1500 level, while real wages, the purchasing capacity of what a man or woman could earn for a day's labour, was at less than a half [147 *pp. 136, 222*]. The effect of all this was the creation of a mass of very poor people, and of serious social strains at the base of society. But the socio-economic changes of the period also encouraged the rise of a stratum of rich yeoman farmers: rising bread prices brought misery for the poor, but they brought enhanced profits for those with a surplus of grain to sell. So the logic of the social and economic changes of the sixteenth and seventeenth centuries, certainly over much of southern and eastern England, was to accentuate pre-existing social stratification. Many villages were increasingly divided between the poor on the one hand, and on the other a loose oligarchy of yeoman farmers, petty gentry, and the more prosperous tradesmen and craftsmen who exercised control as employers, as sources of credit, and through holding such local offices as constable, churchwarden, manorial juror, and overseer of the poor [148 *pp. 102–8*].

Witchcraft in early modern Europe is normally seen as a peasant phenomenon, and in England as in most of the continent the bulk of the
population lived on the land. It is, perhaps, worth pondering on witchcraft in its urban context. What needs to be understood is that England
before the mid-eighteenth century possessed a relatively undeveloped
urban sector: there were few towns of over 10,000 inhabitants, and the
second largest city in the country, Norwich, numbered only 30,000
inhabitants by 1700. The only really large urban centre was London,
growing from perhaps 150,000 inhabitants in 1550 to 375,000 in 1650
and then to 500,000 by 1700. English witchcraft as an urban phenomenon has been little studied, although there is every reason to believe
that in small towns it hardly differed from the witchcraft of the sur-
rounding countryside: the size of most towns hardly makes it possible to
envisage that urban life was qualitatively different from a rural one,
while in any case many town-dwellers were recent immigrants from the
countryside who would have brought rural beliefs with them. Witchcraft
and the occult in early modern London is a subject which awaits, and
would certainly reward, detailed investigation. Scattered references to
accusations against witches, to witch-trials, and to cunning folk suggest
that many beliefs flourishing in the countryside were flourishing in the
capital, and that lower-class Londoners shared many beliefs of contemporary countryfolk. Evidence of magical practitioners in the London area
surfaced in James I's reign during the scandal which accompanied the
divorce of the earl of Essex and his wife and the related scandal sur-
rounding the murder of Sir Thomas Overbury [143], while the successful
career of William Lilly in the mid-seventeenth century suggests the presence of a body of cunning folk and other occult practitioners in the
capital [96].

Community rifts and the uses of anthropology

Cities suffered their stresses in this period, and the lot of the urban poor
was as invidious as that of their rural equivalents. Yet it is to the countryside, and more specifically to rural Essex, which we must return as we
continue our analysis of the dynamics of witchcraft accusation. As we
have noted, in the economically advanced and relatively heavily populated

southern and eastern counties a marked differentiation was growing up in many settlements between richer and poorer villagers. This tendency is of obvious relevance to witchcraft given Macfarlane's finding that the characteristic pattern behind witchcraft accusations was for richer villagers to accuse poorer ones. Macfarlane discovered that a husband's occupation was known for 49 women accused of witchcraft in his Essex sample (the court records of the period usually describe women in terms of their marital status, as spinsters, wives, or widows). Of these 49 husbands, 23 were labourers, eleven husbandmen (farmers of middling fortune), and only four yeomen (the remainder were drawn from a variety of trades: weaver, shoemaker, masons). The alleged victims of witchcraft, or their husbands or fathers, demonstrated a higher average social profile: of the 45 for whom relevant information can be found, sixteen were yeomen, four husbandmen, and a mere four labourers, with the remaining nineteen drawn from a wide variety of trades, the largest group being five sailors [94 *p. 150*]. On this evidence, those accused of witchcraft were most likely to be wives of labourers, those accusing them yeomen farmers or members of their families. There is a complication here, namely that taking a witch, or any criminal, to court in this period cost money (fees had to be paid to the courts' clerical staff), and many of the labouring poor who thought themselves bewitched may have been dissuaded from taking their tormentors to court by the costs of prosecution: but qualitative materials also seem to make it clear that yeoman farmers played a leading role in focusing suspicions of witchcraft and in subsequent prosecutions. Moreover, Macfarlane established that those accused of witchcraft, although poor, usually had a stake in village society: they were not vagrants or the truly destitute but rather people who had lived in their communities for some time, in many cases for all or most of their lives. And, perhaps a regional peculiarity this, Macfarlane's sample demonstrated that the gentry hardly ever figured as victims of witchcraft: witchcraft seemed to be a matter which operated primarily among neighbours.

Macfarlane's interpretation of this pattern of witchcraft accusations was very much informed by his readings into social anthropology. Keith Thomas had, in fact, called for a closer *rapprochement* between the two disciplines in 1963 [151], and from the start it seemed that witchcraft might be a topic which would provide a useful area for discussion between the two disciplines. Again, this was a suggestion which G.L. Kittredge had raised in 1929 [90 *p. 26*], while it was explored more thoroughly in 1958 in a now rather undeservedly forgotten book by G. Parrinder [70]. The underlying logic which might encourage the historian of witchcraft to examine anthropological approaches to the subject is, in its essence, straightforward and attractive. Witchcraft is a very difficult subject for historians to understand, not least because it is a phenomenon which falls outside the immediate experience of most of them. But it is an issue which has been of considerable concern to anthropologists, many of whom have actually observed the operation of witchcraft and sorcery at first hand, and have discussed these matters with both witches and their supposed victims. While a blind acceptance of anthropological models should be eschewed, it would therefore seem to be an attractive idea to examine what anthropologists have written about witchcraft, and ponder on how far their findings and methodologies might offer insights on how witchcraft operated within the popular culture of early modern Europe [72]. And although witchcraft as a topic is now taken more seriously by the generality of British historians than it was when Macfarlane wrote in 1970, anthropology still helps reassure historians of witchcraft that the subject of their study, so often written off as bizarre and marginal by some of their colleagues, does make sense in specific cultural contexts.

Macfarlane was certainly convinced that anthropology offered considerable insights into how Essex villagers thought about witchcraft, and what functions it performed within their culture. In many societies studied by anthropologists, as in Tudor and Stuart England, witchcraft was regarded as the cause of otherwise inexplicable misfortunes, thus both explaining those misfortunes and, by linking them with a human agent, making it possible to do something about them. Moreover, anthropological interpretations which see witchcraft accusations as a means of severing difficult or redundant social relations have obvious resonances for the 'charity refused' model of witchcraft accusations which we shall examine in the next paragraph. But for all of the value which anthropological insights offered Macfarlane, and, to a lesser extent, Keith Thomas, a number of problems remain. Firstly, 'anthropology' is no more a homogeneous discipline than 'history', and both Macfarlane and Thomas were drawing largely on one anthropological tradition, that of the British functionalist school, whose researches were centred on Africa and whose approach to witchcraft was symbolised by E.E. Evans-Pritchard's classic *Witchcraft, Oracles and Magic among the Azande* of 1937. As anthropological critics of Keith Thomas's work pointed out, this school provided only one of the possible approaches to anthropology [139]. Secondly, anthropology, especially as employed by Macfarlane, while excellent in opening up the dynamics of a chronologically limited event, is simply not designed to explain change over long timespans, arguably still one of the major objectives of the historian. Moreover, even early modern England was a more developed society than those which have traditionally formed the subject matter for anthropologists. It had a complex and increasingly dynamic economy, a complex social structure and a fair degree of social mobility, a developed church, and a developed state judicial system. One must express sympathy and admiration for the novelty of Macfarlane and Thomas's approach, and for their major achievement in construct-ing a totally new perspective on the history of witchcraft: nevertheless, it is probably instructive that few historians have followed them in the pursuit of anthropological comparisons.

The 'charity refused' model

One of the reasons for this, as we have hinted, is the feeling that in comparing the tribal societies studied by anthropologists in the first half of the twentieth century like is not being compared with like. Early modern England, we must reiterate, had a developed social structure and a developed economy, two points which are, indeed, central to Macfarlane and Thomas's model of witchcraft accusations. As we have seen, Macfarlane discovered that the most common pattern in his Essex materials was for richer villagers to accuse poorer ones of being witches, and his analysis of this pattern led to his promulgation of what might be described as the 'charity refused' paradigm. The dominant motif, on Macfarlane's reading of the Essex materials, seemed to be for an elderly and comparatively poor woman to request something at the door of one of her more substantial neighbours: some food, some beer, a little money, maybe the chance to do some work. This would be refused, and the woman would either curse the refuser, or go away mumbling threats or ambivalent phrases. A little later, a misfortune would befall the household of the refuser of charity: a child would sicken, farm animals might die, or the head of household himself would be smitten by a strange malady. A connection would be made between this misfortune and the altercation with the elderly woman: thus the misfortune would be ascribed to witchcraft rather than the will of God, natural causes, or simple bad luck [*Docs 6 and 7*].

All of this can be placed very firmly in the economic circumstances of the time. The demographic growth of the period and the resultant pressure on resources meant, as we have suggested, that there were more people around for whom times were hard, and hence they were more likely to seek alms or favours from their neighbours. However, the growth of a more commercial ethic among the yeoman farmers and others at the top of village society meant that they were less likely to regard their poorer neighbours as fit objects for indiscriminate charity. But these farmers and others were in an ambivalent position: despite their commercial hard-headedness, they were also attached to community norms, and hence in what was essentially a transitional socio-economic phase felt uncertain about how to treat the poor. This problem arguably became clearer as the seventeenth century progressed, and the workings of the poor law legislation of 1598 and 1601 helped formalise and stabilise relationships between rich and poor in the local community. But interpreting the misfortunes which came after refusing charity to a poorer neighbour as the result of witchcraft helped overturn any feelings of residual guilt which may have been felt: it was now the malefic witch, not the farmer or member of his household who refused charity, who was the transgressor of community norms.

Clearly, on the basis of the criminal charges levelled against them, what worried people most about witches was *maleficium*, the doing of concrete harm by witchcraft [*Doc. 8*]. English witches, on the strength of assize indictments, were rarely accused of raising storms, blasting the crops, sinking ships at sea, impeding human fertility, or consorting with evil spirits. Taking Essex indictments between 1560 and 1680, it appears that witches were accused of causing the death of 233 humans, the illness of a further 108, while in 80 cases they were accused of harming or killing animals, while a further six were charged with harming other property by witchcraft, this last category including burning down a couple of barns, twenty brewings of beer spoiled, a windmill bewitched, and four gallons of cream prevented from becoming butter [94 *pp. 152–3*].

There are, however, some problems in arguing purely from assize indictments, whose descriptions of acts of witchcraft are formulated in such a way as to gain a conviction under the 1563 and 1604 statutes rather than to furnish later historians with an account of the full range of early modern beliefs about witches. There is a sample of eighteen Elizabethan Essex witches whose activities are described not only in indictments but also in pamphlets, and comparing the two bodies of source materials confirms the suspicion that formal court indictments provide a very selective impression of what witches were meant to do [94 *p. 153*]. The indictments describe 21 cases of death and four of illness being caused to humans, the pamphlets 32 and seventeen respectively; the indictments give three instances when these witches were meant to have bewitched animals, the pamphlets seventeen; and although the indictments mention only one instance of miscellaneous harm caused by witchcraft, burning a barn, the pamphlets record a whole gamut of damage caused by the witches: seven instances of spoiling beer, three of spoiling butter, and other occasions when witches allegedly made cows give blood rather than milk, interfered with the operation of a spinning wheel, and caused a cart to remain immobile. In a sceptical tract published in 1653 the Kentish justice of the peace and political theorist Sir Robert Filmer was to comment of assize judges that 'ordinarily they condemne none for witches, unless they be charged with the murdering of some person' [19 *p. 2*]. Clearly, well before Filmer wrote, people taking witches to court were selective about which of the harms that the witches in question were meant to have caused were actually chosen to furnish the basis for a formal court prosecution. The details of what witches were meant to have done as provided by indictments must, therefore, remain a very imperfect guide to wider beliefs about witches' activities.

Nevertheless, it is clear that, if it was the pact with the devil which the educated theologian held to be central to witchcraft, for the population at large it was *maleficium*. George Gifford, here as elsewhere anxious to replace popular misconceptions about witchcraft with an informed theological interpretation, was quite precise on this point:

> The holy scriptures doe command that witches should be put to death: therein you say right: but if you take it, that the word of God commaundeth they shall not be suffered to live, because they kill men and beastes, or because they send their spirites which possesse men, and torment their bodies, you are much deceived: for you shal never finde, of all that have been tormented and plagued by evill spirites, that the holie Ghoste layeth it upon witches. The causes why they should be put to death are, that they have familiaritie with devils, which are the blasphemous enemies of God. [22 *sig. H1v*]

These words were published in 1593 and the next century was to witness some progress in bringing an informed, theologically sound notion of witchcraft to the population at large. But among the common people it was the harm which witches were thought to do, rather than their pact with the devil, which was to remain the principal reason for worrying about witchcraft.

The identity of witches

Analysis of trial records also gives us a clear impression of who the witches were. The most striking point is, of course, that witches tended overwhelmingly to be women. We have already noted that this point has been made much of by recent writers on witchcraft, and it is a theme to whose wider ramifications we shall return in the next chapter. What needs to be noted here is that English witchcraft, or to be more accurate English witchcraft as represented by Home Circuit assize indictments, was unusual in this respect. The indictments demonstrate that just under 90 per cent of those indicted for witchcraft at the south-eastern assizes were women [100 *p. 108*], which is higher than what might be described as the European average of 80 per cent (it should be remembered that in some parts of Europe the proportion of women charged as witches was much lower). Given that the connection between women and witchcraft has been afforded such a central importance by modern writers [e.g., 86, 89, 97], and was clearly demonstrated by the reality of the witch-trials, it comes as something of a surprise to recognise that the connection between women and witchcraft in the early modern period was something which attracted little attention from contemporaries. Generally, demonological writers regarded the fact that most witches were women as axiomatic, a given factor which only needed to be mentioned briefly, thus reserving more space for what these writers obviously regarded as more interesting and more important issues. William Perkins, to take a typical example, devoted only two paragraphs of his large tract on witchcraft to the problem of women and witchcraft, and made some very stereotyped comments. He observed that

> The woman being the weaker sexe, is sooner intangled by the devill's illusions, with the damnable art, than the man. And in all ages it is found true by experience, that the devill hath more easily and oftner prevailed with women then with men . . . his first temptation in the beginning, was with Eve a woman, and since he pursueth his practice accordingly as making for his advantage. For where he findeth easiest entrance, and best entertainment, thither will he oftnest resort. [36 *pp. 168–9*]

Thus the conventional wisdom was that women were morally and intellectually weaker, and thus more prone to the devil's snares, that this point was demonstrated at a very early stage in human history by Eve, and that, in any case, the objective reality of witch accusations (finding true by experience, as Perkins put it) constantly demonstrated the connection between witchcraft and women. In a sense, the very fact that most demonological writers felt no need to labour the connection demonstrates just how well established it was [*Doc. 9*].

But, as comment from modern historians and some of the more sceptical early modern observers makes clear, it was not any woman who was likely to be accused of witchcraft: in England at least it was, for the most part, elderly (or at least middle-aged) and poor ones. Thus John Gaule, writing in 1646 in the face of the Matthew Hopkins trials, could castigate the attitude by which

> every old woman with a wrinkled face, a furr'd brow, a hairy lip, a gobber tooth, a squint eye, a squeaking voyce, or a scolding tongue, having a rugged coate on her back; a skull-cap on her head; a spindle in her hand, and a dog or cat at her side; is not only suspected, but pronounced for a witch. [21 *pp. 4–5*]

This model of the typical witch does, of course, fit the Macfarlane–Thomas socio-economic paradigm of witchcraft: elderly women were more likely than men to be economically and socially marginalised within the village community. It remains contested how far widows were over-represented among those women accused of witchcraft, but, following this logic of marginalisation, it seems probable that they might be re-garded as a special problem, removed as they were from both the control and the protection which marriage within a patriarchal society would be considered to provide for them.

Many of these elderly or middle-aged women accused of witchcraft had a long-standing reputation for being a witch. Some of the more detailed descriptions of cases, for example that offered by the Yorkshire gentleman Edward Fairfax of the six women who he thought to be bewitching his daughters, demonstrate this point clearly [*Doc. 10*]. Briefer accounts as offered in witnesses' statements or trial pamphlets likewise frequently mention that the accused had a well-established previous reputation as a practitioner of witchcraft, further reinforcement to this point often being furnished by the widespread contemporary belief that witches were prone to inherit their ability to do evil from their mothers. One concomitant of these established reputations was that witches were people you were scared of. This runs through Edward Fairfax's account, and is also demonstrated in George Gifford's analysis of witchcraft beliefs in Essex in the Elizabethan period. Gifford has a countryman named Samuel, one of the characters in his *Dialogue concerning Witches and Witch-craftes*, voice the following sentiments about witches in his locality:

> there be two or three in our towne which I like not, but especially an old woman, I have beene as careful to please her as ever I was to please mine own mother, and to give her ever anon one thing or other, and yet me thinkes shee frownes at me now and then. And I had a hogge which eate his meate with his fellowes and was very well to our thinking over night, and in the morning he was starke dead. My wife had five or six hennes even of late dead. [22 *sig. B1*]

As we construct our interpretations of witchcraft, perhaps especially when we are considering socio-economic explanations, we must be careful not to lose sight of the fact that for most of those who thought themselves to be bewitched the experience was a terrifying one, and the witch a figure who inspired fear and loathing of the deepest nature. On this level, witchcraft, to state a proposition to which we shall return in the next chapter, was very much about power.

Witchcraft and the politics of reputation

But as both Fairfax's and Gifford's comments suggest, suspicions of witch-craft, and the formal accusations to which they could lead, must also be understood within the context of the 'politics of reputation' within which early modern villagers lived. The village community may not have been the static and unchanging 'traditional' society of later sociological myth, but it was very much a face-to-face society, a social microcosm where people knew each other in a multiplicity of roles and where people took an interest in each other's business, a milieu where the 'symbolic credit' of reputation was, in most everyday transactions, as important as financial standing [153]. These local microcosms, as far as we can tell from the available evidence, were also places where people told stories about each other, and where gossip was a major pastime. The conduct of both individuals and households was constantly being subjected to neigh-bourly evaluation, with an awareness of past reputation, for good or ill, constantly being brought into play. Thus when pigs died or children grew ill and a natural explanation seemed insufficient, memories of past acts of witchcraft could be raked up to help inform current matters of neighbourly interest. Yet this type of attack on reputation did not go uncontested. It was not unknown for people who were being called witches by their neighbours to bring defamation suits, especially in the local ecclesiastical courts, against their accusers [128, 146] [Doc. 11]. One suspects that those initiating such litigation might well have been wealthier, and in possession of a higher standing in their communities, than the generality of witches, or perhaps that they had husbands who were willing to stand by them and provide the financial and emotional support needed to fight a court action: but such cases do demonstrate at least one way in which a person suspected of maleficium could use offi-cial channels to defend her or his reputation.

In a surprising number of instances, indeed, it seems that people accused of witchcraft were able to mobilise considerable support within their communities. This very much challenges the standard interpreta-tion of the witch as the victim of simple-minded intolerance or brainless scapegoating, and the witchcraft accusation as the outcome of some sort of tyranny of local opinion. Thus in December 1651 a petition with some 200 signatures was sent to the northern assizes concerning Mary Hickington, 'now a condemned prisoner in Yorke castle for witchcraft'. The petitioners declared that Hickington and her husband (who had served in the parliamentarian forces at Hull) were both of good character, and that the woman had never been suspected of witchcraft or sorcery or any other offences 'not becoming a Christian' [131 *p. 22*]. Another petition, this time signed by 50 members of a suspected witch's community, came from Denby in Yorkshire in 1674. A teenage girl named Mary Moor had accused three people, among them Susan Hinchcliffe and her husband, of witchcraft. The petition stressed Susan Hinchcliffe's good reputation, adding that 'touching the said girle who now informs, some of us could say too much of her, of a quite different nature', and declared the accusation 'gros and groundless (if not malitious)' [132 *p. 23*]. A very similar example, which we know contributed to the acquittal of accused witches, occurred, again in Yorkshire, in 1623. Edward Fairfax, the gentleman who was so concerned over the bewitchment of his daughters, eventually had the women he suspected tried at the assizes. To his dismay they were acquitted, and after the trial Fairfax recorded how

> It hath been told me that one John Dibb, son of Dibb's wife [one of the accused witches] procured a certificate to the judge, that the women were of good fame, and never till that time ill-reported of for witchcraft; and that Henry Graver solicited and induced many persons to set their hands to the same, upon advantage of which certificate such magistrates as are incredulous in these things work their deliverance. [12 *p. 127*]

Fairfax was a gentleman, and indeed a member of one of the most important gentry families in West Yorkshire. Yet even he was unable to secure the conviction of those he thought to be bewitching his daughters in the face of official scepticism and a rallying of community support for the alleged witches.

Such evidence suggests that notions of hegemonic community hostility to the witch may be a little misleading. Well-documented cases show with surprising frequency that opinion about witchcraft accusations within the local community could be very divided. There might be a body within a village, including many of its more substantial inhabitants, who had identified one or several of their neighbours as witches, and were anxious to invoke legal process to counter this problem. But there were often others, both substantial villagers and such local notables as clergymen and gentry, who were cautious about accusations, or who felt moved by ties of kinship or friendship to support the supposed witches. Such factors were at play even during what has frequently, and justifiably, been portrayed as an episode of severe anti-witch hysteria, the period of the Matthew Hopkins witch-hunts. John Stearne, Matthew Hopkins' associate in these hunts, remembered how a powerful resident of Colchester had defended alleged witches in 1645:

> This man, with another who is likewise reported to have been fellow-agent with him in that businesse, and the two chiefest in it, was the cause that some were not questioned in that town: but for his part, I saw him labour and endeavour all he could to keep this woman, whom he so much held withal from her legal trial, and likewise heard him threaten both me and all that had given evidence against her, or informed what manner she had been in her life and conversation, to their knowledge, or as they had heard: yea, as I since have heard, she was condemned at that assize, and by his procurement reprieved. [41 p. 58]

One is left wondering how many other, undocumented, cases there were in which alleged witches were either acquitted, or saved from trial entirely, by the intercession of local notables who were convinced of their innocence. What such examples demonstrate, it must be emphasised, is the inaccuracy of the view which would argue that a person suspected of being a witch would be destined automatically for trial and execution [Doc. 12].

Indeed, the coming of a witchcraft case to trial and the subsequent conviction or acquittal of the witch were frequently affected by existing splits and factions within the local community. One such situation arose in the small port town of Rye in Sussex. This is an exceptionally well-documented case (there are 20,000 words of witnesses' statements) which reveals how witchcraft suspicions might operate against a background of folk beliefs, with fairy lore being especially prominent in this instance [116]. But it has also been argued that this accusation should be understood within the context of social and economic change in Rye. The port was in decline, with a group of traders centred on the town's butchers doing especially badly, although their problems were offset by the relative prosperity of another faction, centred on Rye's brewers, one of whom, Thomas Hamon, was the main victim of the supposed witchcraft. These economic splits, as so often, interacted with religious splits within the town. On a less institutionalised level, it is sometimes possible to discern loose groupings within or around communities who took sides when suspicions of witchcraft were set in motion. Edward Fairfax, for example, noted how the women he suspected of bewitching his daughters 'wanted not both counsellors and supporters of the best. These men at feasts and meetings spread reports and moved doubts, inferring a supposal of coun-terfeiting and practice in the children, and that it was not serious, but a combination proceeding of malice' [12 p. 36]. He noted how at one point he consulted a substantial neighbour, Henry Graver, and the local vicar, Nicholas Smithson, for advice about how to deal with one of the witches, 'but I found myself deceived in that expectation, for these men were great friends to the woman' [12 p. 50]. He also commented of another 'great favourer of the women questioned', Henry Robinson, that 'at this time there is some unkindness and questions of law between us' [12 pp. 93–4]. Once more we are reminded that a successful witchcraft accusa-tion was not a foregone conclusion, and that local enmities, friendship groupings, and faction might work as effectively against the accuser as against the witch.

The complexity of the local issues at play is further revealed by a case involving the gentry as accusers and supposed victims. Macfarlane's research on Essex found little gentry involvement on this level, but evidence from other areas gives a different impression. One of the most celebrated of English witchcraft incidents was that of the witches of Warboys, which led to the execution for witchcraft of Alice and John Samuels and their daughter Agnes in 1593 [34]. Research on the village background reveals that the Samuels were an established local family, a bit rough perhaps (John seems to have been involved in a number of disputes with his neighbours), but reasonably well off, this last point being reinforced by their goods being valued at £40 after their execu-tion. Their accuser, conversely, was Robert Throckmorton, member of a nationally important gentry family who had risen to prominence through service at court and purchase of monastic land, and who were connected through friendship and marriage to other gentry families, notably the locally important Cromwells and the intensely Puritan Pickerings of Northamptonshire. Thus it has been argued that the context for the Warboys case was provided by a clash of ideals about how a community should work: Warboys had essentially been a village run by its local manorial court, where local farming families serving as jurors had controlled matters, but now it had to absorb a nationally networked and religiously innovative gentry family [110]. A not dissimilar situation seems to have obtained a little later at North Moreton in Berkshire (modern local government boundaries changes have now placed it in Oxfordshire) where suspicions of witchcraft led to the trial and acquittal of two women in 1605, and subsequent Star Chamber proceedings against their accusers, Brian Gunter and his daughter Anne [101]. Again, the village was one which was run by substantial farming families through the manorial court, although the incoming gentry family here was headed by a man who was socially and economically aggressive. Bad blood between Brian Gunter and the Gregory family began in May 1598, when Brian Gunter inflicted fatal injuries on two of the Gregorys in the course of a brawl during a village football match. But Gunter, like Robert Throckmorton, had his social connections. Another of his daughters, Susan, was married to the regius professor of theology at Oxford, and in the subsequent court proceedings a number of university men gave evidence in his favour. As both the Warboys and the Gunter cases demonstrate, those making accusations of witchcraft could have horizons far wider than those formed by the boundaries of their village.

That the origins of the Gunter case can be traced to violence at a football match reminds us that the 'charity refused' model of a witchcraft accusation, apparently so powerful in south-eastern England, was not so universally present in other parts of the country. In less economically advanced Yorkshire, for example, cases arising from 'fallings out' when charity was refused existed, but were not as pervasive as in socially and economically precocious Essex [131]. Indeed, it is possible to find an enormous range of antagonisms, personal feuds, and areas of competitiveness underlying a witchcraft accusation. We have noted the tale of Brian Gunter and football violence. Mary Smith, executed for witchcraft at Kings Lynn in Norfolk in 1616, had fallen out with her fellow townsfolk over the price of cheese in the local market [39]. Thomas Darling, a godly youth allegedly bewitched in 1597, had supposedly attracted the odium of his tormentor, Alice Gooderidge, when he inadvertently broke wind in her presence [15]. And, as we shall see when we re-open our discussion of witchcraft and gender in the next chapter, a large number of witchcraft trials arose from disputes between women over access to domestic social space, or over what the period would have regarded as the most female of concerns, the care of children. Ongoing investigation to the background to trials suggests that virtually every form of conflict might lead to an accusation of witchcraft [55, 114].

This conclusion means that it is sometimes possible to find persons accused of malefic witchcraft who bear scant resemblance to the normal witch stereotype. One such was William Godfrey of New Romsey in Kent, tried for witchcraft in 1617 [115]. Godfrey was very different from the typical witch: his age, 47, was right, but against this must be set the fact that he was male, and comfortably off, married with two children, a substantial farmer living in a two-storey house, keeping a servant, sufficiently well off to pay poor rate and of sufficient social standing locally to serve his community both as a juror and as a militiaman. Godfrey was the subject of a number of witchcraft accusations. These were apparently initiated by William Clarke, a near neighbour who was roughly similar to Godfrey in age and status, and who alleged that after a dispute caused by Godfrey's ducks straying on to his land, his lambs became lame and his wife was unable to turn butter into cheese. John and Susan Barker remembered problems with Godfrey dating back to 1609, when they had rented his house. They suffered a series of lisasters which they attributed to the residence being haunted or bewitched. A similar tale was told by two other previous tenants, William and Margaret Holton, who lived in the house between 1613 and 1615, while other neighbours testified to Godfrey's long-standing reputation as a witch. Godfrey had earlier been implicated in stealing a lamb, and was possibly involved in other disputes with his neighbours. As the Godfrey case reminds us, it was not just poor elderly women who were perceived as troublesome neighbours, and who might also be perceived as witches.

Focusing on trial documents or trial pamphlets thus opens up many aspects of witchcraft. Above all, this process demonstrates how the witch-trial was an event where beliefs about witchcraft at a variety of social levels came into play: those of the villagers who were both the suspected witches and their accusers, and who formed the juries which tried witches; of the local notables who interested themselves in witchcraft cases; and of the judges presiding over the courts. The great historian of Scottish witchcraft, Christina Larner, commented that it was the state's interest in witchcraft, expressed via the witch-trial, which made the witch 'a transformed creature who began her career in the farmyard as an enemy of her neighbours, and ended it in the court as a public person, as an enemy of God and the godly society' [64 *p. 5*]: these words are equally telling for England. But as this chapter has demonstrated, the trials and the suspicions and accusations of varying levels of intensity which preceded them provide all sorts of keys to the nature of witchcraft as a cultural phenomenon in early modern society. Such questions as who the suspected witches were, who accused them, where both accuser and accused were located in the local social structure, and how their neighbours and locally influential people reacted as a witchcraft accusation unfolded: all of these are matters which can be illustrated by trial records, by other official documentation, and by the pamphlets which were written about trials. What we must do next, however, is go beyond the dynamics of formal accusation, and ask further questions about the workings of witchcraft and witchcraft beliefs in the broader social and cultural context.

4

Witch beliefs: the broader spectrum

The trials of alleged witches, as described in both court records and contemporary pamphlets, thus constitute an area of central concern to the historian of witchcraft, not least, as we have suggested, because criminal court archives and pamphlets describing witch-trials remain two of the major bodies of source material upon which a study of wider aspects of witch beliefs in early modern England might be based. It is, indeed, upon some of these wider aspects that we will now focus our attention. We have already examined some of the educated beliefs, especially those of learned theologians, and this chapter will carry us in another direction, towards the beliefs of the population at large. What should be remembered, however, is that here as elsewhere in the culture of the period, 'elite' and 'popular' beliefs did not operate in isolation, and were not hermetically sealed from each other [120]. The views of the educated and the population at large interacted, the one constantly informing and modifying the other. It is therefore sometimes possible to see how what we might describe as popular ideas about witchcraft connected not just with the more general popular belief system, but also with the elite mentalities and, in particular, with the official religious beliefs of the period. As we shall see, the issues arising from these aspects of witchcraft history are frequently very complex, and currently many of them await more detailed research, more rigorous analysis, and more sophisticated conceptualisation.

Counter magic

The better-documented court cases, as well as a number of other sources, contain references to informal counter action against witchcraft which frequently preceded a formal accusation of witchcraft at court, and, in rather more cases one suspects, served as an alternative to formal prosecution. Demonologists insisted that the only proper remedies for witchcraft were taking the suspected witch before the authorities for trial, or adopting prayer and fasting, in effect suffering witchcraft with the same patience with which Job suffered the afflictions heaped upon him. But taking a witch to court took time and money (perhaps too much money for the bulk of the population), while, as theologians never ceased to complain, ordinary countryfolk suffering from misfortune showed a marked unwillingness to adopt a Job-like patience in the face of adversity. The English therefore demonstrated a variety of informal methods for dealing with witchcraft.

Although such remedies might be thought to be counter-productive, it was not unknown for witches to be threatened or beaten by their supposed victims, while the West Yorkshire nonconformist Oliver Heywood noted an instance in 1667 when violence against a witch was taken to its logical conclusion, and three men from Wakefield killed a woman they thought to be a witch (the three were hanged for murder, a demonstration of the attitude of officialdom to such acts of violence against witches [145, vol. 3 p. 100]). Most commonly, violence against the witch took the form of a ritualised scratching to draw blood from the witch (scratching the witch's forehead was thought to be especially efficacious), the belief being that such action destroyed the witch's power over her victim. There were other ways in which harming the witch was thought to have this effect. Thus in the course of the Warboys affair, Lady Susan Cromwell, demonstrating the existence of such beliefs among leading gentry families, in hopes of alleviating the sufferings of the Throckmorton children cut hair from the head of the suspected witch Alice Samuel, and threw it in the fire [34 *sig. E5*]. Burning the thatch from a witch's roof was also thought to ensure beneficial results. Those suffering from witchcraft or their associates could make a witch cake, in which urine from the bewitched person was mixed with grain of some kind to make a cake, and then burnt on the fire, thus, by sympathetic magic, afflicting the urinary–genital system of the supposed witch, and forcing her to reveal herself when she came to find the source of her affliction. Bewitched cattle could be burnt. This practice might have some practical effect in breaking the chain of infection among sick animals, although at least one person trying this remedy got himself into severe trouble. John Crushe of Hawkwell in Essex was, in 1624, presented before the local archdeacon's court after his efforts to burn a bewitched lamb alive set fire to the common one Sunday and disrupted the parish's religious devotions [94 *p. 286*]. And, of course, if you thought yourself bewitched you could go to cunning folk for advice.

There was also a folklore around proving a suspected person was a witch. Edward Fairfax noted a relevant practice when he invoked the assistance of a justice of the peace during the bewitchment of his two daughters in the early 1620s. The justice had presided over a meeting between the elder daughter and one of the suspected witches, and told Fairfax in private 'that he would try if Thorp's wife were a witch, by causing her to say the Lord's Prayer, for if she were a witch, he said, that in the repetition of the prayer she could not say the words "forgive us our trespasses"' [12 *p. 87*]. A rather more dramatic method of establishing proof, and one which remains firmly lodged in modern ideas on witchcraft history, was the swimming test. This involved stripping suspects to their shift, tying them left toe to right thumb and right toe to left thumb, passing a line under their armpits, and throwing them into a pond or river. If they floated, it was thought they were witches: water was a pure element, and hence would reject anything as impure as an agent of Satan. If they sank, conversely, it demonstrated innocence, and they would be swiftly removed from the water by men hanging on to the ends of the rope under their armpits. This practice is one which, in a mythologised form, is widely known about in the modern world, and has been conflated erroneously with the use of the ducking stool against witches. In fact, the swimming test came late to England, being first recorded as an obviously novel practice in a pamphlet of 1613 [50]. It was never a part of official process against witches: a few justices of the peace may have gone along with it, but judges were hostile to the swimming test, and many clergymen regarded it as another of those undesirable popular usages which they so consistently decried when discussing witchcraft. It was, in any case, rarely recorded in the seventeenth century.

Swimming was not the only form of unofficial counter action which attracted the odium of clerical commentators: generally, all of these practices were seen as being without scriptural basis, and hence as ungodly as malefic witchcraft itself [*Doc. 13*]. The views of the godly were stated succinctly by Edward Fairfax, advised by his neighbours to use such practices to help ease his daughters' afflictions:

> I was often moved to seek help by some of these means, especially by the scratching, which was urged to me as a remedy ordained of God, but I could never believe it to be so, for I well knew that God is not tied to form and circumstances . . . we left therefore their charms, tongs, and scratchings to them that put confidence in them, and the devil who devised them; and only relied upon the goodness of God and invoked his help, without tempting him by prescribing the means, but attended his mercy which he hath not witholden from us, so that we are not disappointed in our hope. [12 *pp. 88–9*]

Fairfax, as a well-educated and godly member of the gentry, was probably better equipped than most to reject informal counter-measures and place his trust in prayer: for the bulk of the population this would have been an impossibly austere remedy. Something guaranteeing rapid results, and possibly a degree of personal satisfaction, was seen as more desirable.

One such remedy, attractive to the bulk of the population, but rejected by the godly and those advising them, was seeking the advice and help of cunning folk. Fairfax, if we may stay with this source, noted that in his part of Yorkshire witches were thought to be very active, and that those who thought they had suffered losses through witchcraft 'would go to those they call wisemen, and these wizards teach them to burn young calves alive and the like' [12 *p. 35*]. On 23 November 1621, at an early stage in his daughters' troubles he recorded how 'I was in the kitchen with many of my family [i.e. household, including servants], and there were some speeches made about charmers and lookers on (as the rude people call them) and the names of many that were reckoned up who were thought to be skillful therein' [12 *p. 42*]. This impression of cunning folk being widely known in their area, and having reputations which were widely discussed locally, is confirmed by George Gifford's portrayal of witchcraft beliefs in Essex some 30 years before Fairfax wrote. In his *Dialogue concerning Witches and Witchcraftes* Gifford has one of his characters ask 'have you any cunning man hereabout, that doth help'. The reply came that 'there is one they say, here a twenty miles of[f] at T.B., which hath helpe many . . . there is also a woman at R.H. five and twenty miles hence, that hath a great name, and a great resort there is dayly unto her'. The character expressing these sentiments was able to cite both his own experiences and those of people he knew to confirm the efficacy of the advice and remedies offered by these two magical practitioners [22 *sig. B1*].

The fullest analysis of cunning folk yet made, that based on Essex materials carried out by Alan Macfarlane, confirms the impression of their pervasiveness created in the writings of Fairfax and Gifford. On the strength of the Essex records, Macfarlane was able to demonstrate that in the Elizabethan period 'nowhere in Essex was there a village more than ten miles from a known cunning man. The county was covered by a network of magical practitioners' [94 *p. 120*]. In Elizabethan Essex as elsewhere, cunning folk carried out a number of useful services. They helped find stolen goods, gave servant girls in particular advice about future husbands, provided folk medicine for the sick, and helped people identify those who were bewitching them and gave the supposedly be-witched advice about how to deal with their tormentors. The techniques used varied from practitioner to practitioner [*Doc. 14*]. Verbal spells and charms were frequently employed, the fact that these were often bastard-ised versions of Latin Catholic prayers adding further to the unease of Protestant clerical commentators. Such charms might also be written on paper, and were sometimes worn in an amulet around the client's neck. Herbal remedies, often in conjunction with charms, were widely used for the benefit of the sick. Shears might be balanced on a sieve, and the direction of their turning used as a divinatory device. There was also the use of more advanced techniques, with a few literate cunning folk includ-ing books among their paraphernalia, this in itself a sign of knowledge and power in an age when most people were unable to read. Devices like the crystal ball of the modern fortune teller were occasionally used by cunning folk: Gifford had one of his characters describe how a neighbour consulted a cunning man about witchcraft, 'and told him hee suspected an old woman in the parish', the cunning man, as was probably frequently the case, telling the client what he wanted to know when 'he shewed him her in a glasse' [22 *sig. B1*]. References to cunning folk are numerous, and reveal that their practices were very varied. Given that such people were thought of as beneficial by the bulk of the population, and were therefore unlikely to be reported to the authorities, these practitioners of 'good' magic must have been much more numerous than the historical record suggests.

What surviving references to cunning folk do demonstrate, however, is that a very high proportion of them were male: maybe 90 per cent of malefic witches in England were female, but a majority of known cunning folk were men. In 1648 John Stearne, at the end of his tract's discussion of why so many witches were women, commented that 'women therefore without question exceed men, especially of the hurting witches; but for the other [i.e., good witches], I have knowne more men, and have heard such as have gone to them say, almost generally they bee men, and so likewise finde them to be so in authors, which speake of such' [41 *p. 11*]. Macfarlane's Essex sample bears this out: he provides a list of 63 cunning folk whose names are known, of whom some 44 were men [94 *pp. 117–18*]. The issue needs more research, but there is a sense in which the more elaborate a cunning person's techniques or equipment (book possession maybe being a major consideration here) the more likely they were to be male. Conversely, some striking exceptions to this assertion can be found. Sir William Holcroft, an Essex justice of the peace who in 1687 investigated a gang of itinerant fortune tellers who were sleeping rough in his area, found that one of them, a woman named Ann Watts, owned a number of books, among them Cornelius Agrippa's *Occult Philosophy*, Scot's *Discoverie of Witchcraft*, a 'tutor to astrology', and a work by that prolific almanac writer, John Gadbury [152 *pp. 86–7*].

Wider beliefs and the role of the devil

As references to cunning folk constantly remind us, lore concerning witchcraft connected with a much broader universe of popular beliefs. There was a lively acceptance of the existence of the spirit world, with references to ghosts and poltergeists being especially frequent. There was

a widespread belief in the importance of prophecy, a belief which sometimes got those professing it into serious trouble in a period when the
regime might regard prophecies about the deaths of monarchs or other
major changes in affairs of state as treasonable. There was also astrology.
The roots of this obviously lay in educated culture, but a popular astrology
was spread through almanacs, and at least some cunning folk affected
astrological knowledge, or at least astrological phraseology, and bought
books on astrology, to help bolster their professional image. More firmly
entrenched, perhaps, and certainly more traditional, were fairy beliefs.
Today, fairies are relegated to the world of children's stories (the con-
notations of the term 'fairy tale' are instructive) and are regarded as small
and benevolent. This was not the case in early modern England, where
there was a powerful folklore which saw fairies as active, large, and
frequently mischievous and sometimes malevolent beings [102 *pp. 607–
14*]. Educated opinion might have been rejecting fairy beliefs, and even
among the population at large such beliefs, by the later seventeenth
century at least, may have been regarded as something most appropriate
for servant girls and children: yet many village wizards and cunning folk
claimed to be in touch with the fairies, while John Webster, a north
country pastor-cum-physician who published a sceptical book on witchcraft in 1677, noted that in Yorkshire 'fairy-taken' was a synonym for
being haunted or bewitched [49 *pp. 323–4*].

The most powerful of malign beings was, of course, the Devil. This
said, it remains clear that research is needed on popular notions of the
Devil, which may well have been different, in some respects at least,
from those of learned theologians. Most relevant for our present discus-
sions, however, is the issue of how far the demonological emphasis on
the centrality of the demonic pact in the problem of witchcraft came to
be accepted among the population at large. English witchcraft beliefs
have frequently been portrayed as being less concerned with this issue
than beliefs held in Lowland Scotland or parts of continental Europe,
where the peasantry had been more effectively schooled in what the age
would have regarded as the correct theological position on such matters.
While it is true that *maleficium* lay at the core of English witch beliefs,
there is every indication that from the early seventeenth century ideas,
albeit folklorised, of the demonic pact were entering popular notions

about witches. Edward Fairfax could state in 1622 that 'of these contracts with the devil the reports both by books and traditions be infinite' [12 *p. 88*], and it is certain that around that date they were certainly becoming more frequent. Several of those executed for witchcraft in the famous Lancashire trials of 1612 confessed to entering into a pact with the devil, and the notion was clearly there in the trials of 1633–34 in the same area [*Doc. 15*]. By the time of the Matthew Hopkins trials in the 1640s, such ideas, possibly helped along by the interrogation techniques used during this episode, were firmly planted in the eastern counties. It is possible to reconstruct 110 narratives of witchcraft from the Hopkins period, of which 63 mention the Devil. Many of these make reference to something rarely noted before, sexual intercourse between the witch and the devil, an encounter which those confessing to have experienced it normally found unsatisfactory [100 *pp. 134–5*]. By 1682, when Temperance Lloyd, Susanna Edwards and Mary Trembles were tried and executed for witchcraft at Exeter, the notion of the satanic pact was firmly established in the minds of those interrogating the suspected witches and, on the strength of their confessions, in the minds of the convicted women themselves [31, 43, 45]. Here as in the Hopkins trials, leading questions from interrogators probably helped the supposed witches fashion an account of meeting the Devil based on a growing folklore about such matters. And it was, indeed, Hopkins' associate John Stearne who gave an intriguing clue as to how the Devil might enter the popular consciousness in an increasingly Christianized England: 'I have heard many of them [i.e. confessing witches] say', he claimed, 'that the Devil hath inticed them to witchcraft by some sermons they have heard preached; as when ministers will preach of the power of the devil' [41 *p. 59*].

If the Devil made only slow progress from being a peripheral figure in English witchcraft beliefs, it is not surprising that the great occasion when the Devil met witches, the sabbat, was a phenomenon which was only rarely alluded to in sources dealing with witchcraft in England. A massive lore about the sabbat was constructed by continental demonological writers, with witches flying to the sabbat by night, dancing obscenely when they arrived there, feasting on noxious repasts which frequently featured the exhumed bodies of newborn babies, reporting their misdeeds to the devil, and indulging in sexual orgies in which they, the Devil, and attendant demons participated eagerly. Little of this can be found among the witch beliefs of the lower orders in England, and even English demonological writers, like many other Protestant writers on witchcraft, do not seem to have been much concerned with the sabbat. This makes such references as there are to the sabbat in English sources all the more intriguing. Obviously, it is unsurprising that it should be thought that witches might meet occasionally to compare notes on their activities and discuss their techniques, and meetings of this type were clearly envisaged in a pamphlet describing the trial of a small group of witches at Windsor in 1579 [38]. The description of the 1612 Lancashire trials makes several mentions of the alleged witches in that case coming together at the Malkin Tower, but the issue here seems to have been discussing tactics in the face of growing suspicions rather than a sabbat proper [37]. That some ideas of meetings between the Devil and witches were in circulation is demonstrated by Edward Fairfax in 1622, when one of his bewitched daughters, Helen, came across an outdoor meeting of the women supposed to be bewitching her where roast beef was being consumed with the devil sitting at the head of the table [12 *pp. 107–8*].

A little later two other references, from different ends of the country, suggest that a folklore about the sabbat had been established. In 1638 a Devon justice of the peace took depositions about a young girl who, among other ideas on witchcraft, had the notion that every Midsummer Eve 'those that would be witches must meet the divell upon a hill and that there the divell would licke them and that place was black' [100 *p. 77*]. A few years earlier, however, something much more like the sabbat had been recorded in the confessions made by some of those suspected to be witches during the Lancashire scare of 1633–34. Elements of the image of the sabbat constructed then were present in the fullest description of the sabbat we have from an English source, that given in a series of depositions given by a woman called Anne Armstrong to the Northumberland justices in 1673 [*Doc. 16*]. The sabbat may not have been a central aspect of English witchcraft, but these and other references to the phenomenon do point to broad popular traditions on the subject, while in Armstrong's case at least it is possible that English beliefs were in some measure affected by ideas on the sabbat that came across the border from Scotland.

If notions of the demonic pact were less well established in England than in some other territories, and if evidence for the belief in the sabbat is fragmentary, the acceptance of the reality of demonic possession was very well established [93, 101, 105]. The notion that demons could enter the human body was current in the ancient world, and was accepted and reinforced by Christian theologians in the middle ages. The heightened tension over matters religious which followed the Reformation made the phenomenon all the more significant. Catholics and Protestants might differ on how best to help the afflicted persons, with the Catholic rite of exorcism being considered as just a piece of popish mummery by Protestants. But theologians on both sides of the religious divide were convinced of the reality of demonic possession, and were equally convinced of the importance of individual instances of the phenomenon. This importance was heightened by the general acceptance among educated Christians of the belief that they were living in the period immediately before the end of the world and Christ's second coming. Given this premise, it was unsurprising that that most worldly of creatures, the devil, should become hyperactive in his assaults on God's creatures. The body of the demoniac, writhing, contorting, going into trances, vomiting foreign objects, entering into dialogues with the demons inhabiting it, and screaming obscenities at the clergymen who were gathered around the sufferer's bed, therefore became regarded as a literal battleground between the forces of good and evil [133].

The scepticism which had been developed in the upper reaches of the Church of England hierarchy around 1600 acted as some sort of inhibition on the uncritical acceptance of the reality of demonic possession cases in clerical circles, but belief in demonic possession remained widespread. For the historian, however, reconstructing attitudes to the phenomenon in early modern England is complicated by the contemporary tendency to conflate possession with bewitchment. Obviously people could be possessed by demons without human assistance, but more commonly witches seem to have been regarded as responsible for sending spirits into the body of the possessed person, and it is not unusual to find references to people being 'bewitched or possessed', demonstrating that the two forms of affliction were regarded, in their symptoms at least, as almost interchangeable. These symptoms usually ran to a culturally-determined pattern: it was obviously widely known how a possessed person would act. Thus we find two women from West Ham in Essex tried by the Court of Star Chamber for counterfeiting possession in 1621 [100 *p. 193*], while a few years earlier in another case which led to Star Chamber proceedings, Anne Gunter, a young woman from Berkshire who simulated being possessed, claimed that she had read the tract describing the suffering of the Throckmorton girls at Warboys and based her simulations on what she read there [101 *pp. 7–8*]. Cultural patterning also probably lay behind the frequency with which the allegedly possessed were children or adolescents: many of them were subjected to the demanding regimes of godly households, and it is possible to sense that in many cases, consciously or unconsciously, the role of demoniac gave them an excuse for what was in effect licensed misbehaviour [133]. The phenomenon of demonic possession is a fascinating one, highlighting as it does the problems for both modern and contemporary observers in trying to discern what medical problems may have been afflicting some of those who thought themselves to be suffering from occult malevolence. Certainly the details given in such cases where we have full descriptions of the physical symptoms suffered by the demoniac can be very alarming [*Doc. 17*].

Familiars and the witch's mark

Demonic possession was to be found all over western and central Europe in the sixteenth and seventeenth centuries. More uniquely English was the familiar spirit, the half-animal, half-demon beings that most witches in England were thought to own. The origins of these imaginary creatures remain elusive. What is obvious is that they came in very rapidly at about the same time as the 1563 statute. In 1566 the first pamphlet describing an English witch-trial was published, purporting to recount the story of the trial of three women at the assizes at Chelmsford in Essex. The pamphlet includes the confession of Elizabeth Francis, who told how, at the age of twelve, she was initiated into witchcraft by her grandmother, who *inter alia* gave her a familiar in the shape of a tabby cat. The cat, which Francis had to feed on bread and milk, was called Satan, and promised her that she should have goods in return for her renunciation of God and her giving her soul to the cat in return for a few drops of blood. Obviously we have here something very close to the satanic pact [17]. Also in 1566, however, a Dorsetshire wizard called John Walsh was examined before the bishop of Exeter. Walsh's confession, made in response to a number of specific questions put to him, included a number of statements about familiars. The most important familiar was one which, in the approved fashion of the educated magician, Walsh had raised with the aid of a book which had been passed on to him by Robert Drayton, a priest who had taught Walsh the occult arts. But it is obvious from the questions put to Walsh and from his answers, although these latter were often negative or evasive, that both he and those interrogating him were aware of a wider set of beliefs about familiars. Walsh was also clearly immersed in fairy lore, and claimed to be in touch with the fairies, with whom he talked on hills in Dorsetshire [18].

After these early references, familiars crop up with regularity in English witchcraft cases. They seem to constitute the one great peculiarity in English witchcraft beliefs, secondary literature at least suggesting that equivalent beings figured very rarely in the ideas about witchcraft held in other parts of Europe. Moreover, the familiar spirit remains one of the relatively unexplored problems of English witchcraft history, although they clearly constitute an intriguing subject worthy of a full-scale study. They were not much noted before the two 1566 pamphlets, when they seem to arrive from nowhere in a fully developed form. Beliefs about the familiars were, however, varied. Elizabethan pamphlets show some familiars being sent by witches to do evil on their behalf, while other familiars merely gave advice. Some familiars were described by confessing witches as fearsome creatures, others seemed to regard them almost as pets. What is as yet uncertain is where the notion of the familiar came from. There is occasionally a sense that familiars were cognate with fairies, and it is possible that some beliefs about familiars were shaped by fairy lore. Also, as we have noted with John Walsh's confession, the familiar of the popular imagination may well have been a folklorised version of the spirits supposedly raised by late medieval and early modern practitioners of learned magic. The origins of the familiar might, conversely, be traceable to notions of animal demons found in classical literature. It is clear that detailed investigation into the phenomenon of familiars is currently one of the most urgent items on the agenda for future research into English witchcraft history.

Familiars were supposed to suck blood from witches, and the English version of the witch's mark became regarded as the place from whence the blood was sucked [Doc. 18]. The identification of this mark became one of the most definite proofs of witchcraft in England. At first there was some uncertainty about where the mark might most normally be located, and in early trials (like the 1566 Essex one) we find familiars sucking the witch's blood from their faces, their thighs or their arms. But by the early seventeenth century the mark was normally discovered in the pudenda or anus of female witches, the fact that the familiar sucked from so private a place possibly adding a sexual dimension to the witch's relationship with her familiar. Contemporary notions of modesty made it undesirable that men be involved in searching for identifying the witch's mark, so teams of women, with a greater or lesser degree of official input and usually including a midwife or two to provide appropriate expertise, would be appointed as searchers [132 pp. 108–12] [Doc. 19]. The mark was most often identified as a teat or similar protuberance, and, as contemporaries were well aware of natural explanations for such phenomena, those giving evidence about witches' marks were usually at pains to stress that what they had found could only be unnatural.

The dynamics of accusation

The image of confused and elderly women undergoing intimate body searches is one which reinforces the modern assumption that those accused of witchcraft were somehow the victims of ignorance and bigotry. Such a notion would have received little sympathy from those who thought that they, their cattle, or their children had been afflicted by witchcraft. For such people, the witch was a frightening figure whose malice could sometimes be deployed with terrifying speed, efficacy, and unpredictability. John Law, giving evidence in the 1612 Lancashire trials, described how he had been bewitched by Alison Device:

> He deposeth and saith, that about the eighteenth of March last past, hee being a pedler, went with his packe of wares at his back thorow [i.e., through] Colne-field: where unluckily he met with Alizon Device, now prisoner at the barre,

who was very earnest for pinnes, but he would give her none; whereuppon she seemed to be very angry; and when hee was past her, hee fell downe lame in great extremitie; and afterwards by meanes he got into an ale-house in Colne, neere unto the place where hee was first bewitched. [37 *sig. R4v*]

Law lay there 'in great paine, not able to stirre either hand or foote', and was still so seriously afflicted that he was unable to follow his trade when he gave evidence in court a few months later.

We know nothing about Law's previous relationship with Device, although the tenor of his statement suggests that he did know the woman, and hence may have had an idea that she had a pre-existing reputation as a witch. Sometimes, of course, suspicions that an illness or misfortune was attributable to witchcraft emerged slowly, the sufferer being loth to come to such a conclusion. But cases like Law's, with bewitchment following very rapidly after what was often a very minor altercation, were also very frequent. Conceptions of how the witch performed this malice were confused and in any case hard to document. Sometimes the malice was conveyed through a gift, and children in particular might recount how they had been afflicted after accepting an apple or a piece of bread and butter from the supposed witch. The witch might also work her magic after acquiring a piece of clothing or some other property of her victim. Most often, however, words were the medium through which *maleficium* worked. There were the mumbled threats uttered after one of those refusals of charity which, in the south-east at least so often formed the background to a witchcraft accusation. Conversely, fear of bewitchment could follow ambivalent or even friendly words. But in a period when the efficacy of cursing was widely believed in, and when verbal violence in the form of scolding was widely recognised as a form of community disruption, the witch's words were thought to have a special power.

The dramatic and dynamic aspects of a witchcraft accusation were demonstrated when, as was frequently the case, the witch was made to confront her victim in hopes of either gaining a confession, or engineering a situation where a reconciliation might be effected. Such a confrontation took place in the case of John Law, whom, as we have seen, Alison Device had bewitched so suddenly. His son, Abraham, also gave evidence. On finding his father sick, and on hearing him accuse Device of bewitching him, Abraham Law made search after the said Alison, and having found her, brought her to his said father yesterday being the nine & twentieth of this instant March; whose said father in the hearing of this examinate and divers others did charge the said Alison to have bewitched him, which the said Alison confessing did aske this examinate's said father forgiveness upon her knees for the same; whereupon this examinate's father accordingly did forgive her. [37 *sig. S1v*]

Such incidents, with an arranged meeting before witnesses between the alleged witch and her supposed victim resulting in mutual pledges of forgiveness and what was in effect a confession on the part of the witch, were not uncommon. Unfortunately, in this case the meeting did not result in the alleviation of John Law's sufferings. Alison Device was asked in court if she 'could helpe the poore pedler to his former strength and health', but answered that neither she nor any other of the witches then accused could do so.

Witchcraft and the female sphere

Yet, as the story of Alison Device's bewitching of John Law reminds us, this ability to do harm by occult means was something which was attributed with overwhelming frequency to women. As we have already noted, the connection between women and witchcraft is currently one of the most discussed aspects of the subject yet remains one of the most puzzling. Again as we have noted, a model which would interpret this connection purely in terms of the male dominance of women is one which it is difficult to sustain. The detailed examination of relevant cases suggests a more complex situation. The crucial issue is the frequency with which women were involved not just as alleged witches, but also as those involved in accusing or giving evidence against witches [121, 130 *pp. 112–13*, 132]. This can be illustrated by a typical if admittedly small sample of twenty relatively well-documented cases from seventeenth-century Yorkshire [130]. These provide a total of 30 suspected witches, who conform to our statistical expectations in that all but three of them were women, and the three males were all either married to or sons of suspected witches. But of the adults who claimed to have been victims of witchcraft, 22 were men and 21 women, while of those giving evidence about witches, nineteen were men and 27 women, this in a period when

¶The ende and laſt confeſſion of mother Waterhouſe at her death, whiche was the xxix. daye of July.

Anno. 1566.

Mother waterhouſe.

IF yꝛſte (beinge redi pꝛepared to receiue her death) ſhe confeſſed earneſtly that ſhee had bene a wytche and vſed ſuche execrable ſoꝛcerye the ſpace of. xv. yeres, and had don many abhominable dede, the which ſhe repented earneſtely & vnfaynedly, and deſyred almyghty God foꝛgeuenes in that ſhe had abuſed hys moſt holy name by

I her

1. An image of Agnes Waterhouse, hanged for witchcraft in 1566, taken from the first English witch-trial pamphlet, *The Examination and Confession of certaine Wytches at Chensforde in the Countie of Essex, before the Queenes Maiesties Judges, the xxvi day of July Anno 1566* (London, 1566) (Lambeth Palace Library, shelfmark 1587.12 5).

The most wonderfull

and true storie, of a certaine Witch
named *Alse Gooderige of Stapen hill,*
who was arraigned and conuicted at Darbie
at the *Assises there.*

As also a true report of the strange torments of Thomas
Darling, *a boy of thirteene yeres of age, that was pos-*
sessed by the Deuill, *with his horrible fittes and terri-*
ble Apparitions by him vttered at Burton vpon
Trent *in the Countie of* Stafford, *and of his maruel-*
lous deliuerance.

Printed at **London** for **I.O** 1597.

2. Witchcraft pamphlets often contained a strong theological message along with
their narratives of witchcraft. Here the title page from a pamphlet of 1597, dealing
with a case of supposed witchcraft in Derbyshire, is illustrated with a depiction of
the ungodly, among them a Roman Catholic friar being tormented by demons in
Hell (Lambeth Palace Library, shelfmark 1597.15).

DAEMONOLOGIE, IN
FORME OF A DIALOGVE.

FIRST BOOKE.

ARGVMENT.
*The exord of the whole. The description of
Magie in speciall.*

CHAP. I. ARGVMENT.
Proued by the Scripture, that these vnlawfull arts in genere, *haue
bene and may be put in practise.*

PHILOMATHES and EPISTEMON
reason the matter.

PHILOMATHES.

I Am surely very glad to haue met with you this day : for I am of opinion, that ye can better resolue me of some thing, whereof I stand in great doubt, nor any other whomwith I could haue met.

EPI. In what I can, that ye like to speir at me, I will willingly and freely tell my opinion, and if I proue it not sufficiently, I am heartily content that a better reason carry it away then.

PHI. What thinke ye of these strange newes, which now onely furnishes purpose to all men at their meeting : I meane of these Witches ?

EPI. Surely they are wonderfull: And I thinke so cleare and plaine confessions in that purpose, haue neuer fallen out in any aage or countrey.

PHI. No question if they be true, but thereof the Doctours doubts.

EPI. What part of it doubt ye of?

PHI.

3. Despite his reputation as a witch-hunter and demonologist, James VI of Scotland took a generally sceptical view of witchcraft accusations among his southern subjects after his accession to the English throne in 1603. His tract on witchcraft, *Daemonologie*, first published at Edinburgh in 1597, was, however, to be frequently cited by English writers on witchcraft, the fact that so eminent a person had written a work of demonology providing support for adherents of a belief in the reality of witchcraft. This is the title page of the work as it appeared in *The Workes of the most high and mightie Prince Iames: by the Grace of God, King of Great Britaine, France and Ireland, Defender of the Faith &c* (London, 1616) (University of York Library).

Witches Apprehended, Examined and Executed, for notable villanies by them committed both by Land and Water.

With a strange and most true triall how to know whether a woman be a Witch or not.

Printed at London for *Edward Marchant*, and are to be sold at his shop ouer against the Crosse in Pauls Church-yard. 1613.

4. During the seventeenth and eighteenth centuries suspected witches were sometimes subjected to what was known as the swimming test, the idea being that if they floated, it demonstrated their guilt, on the grounds that water was a 'pure' element which would reject anything as ungodly as a witch. The practice, which was generally frowned upon by officialdom, continued to be used by the population at large long after the repeal of the witchcraft statutes in 1736. This illustration comes from the title page of a 1613 pamphlet which includes one of the earliest descriptions of swimming (Bodleian Library, University of Oxford, title page from 4°E17 Art(11)).

The feuerall Notorious and

levvd Coufnages of I o н n VV e s t, and A l i c e VV e s t, falfely called the
King and Queene of Fayries.

Practifed very lately both in this Citie, and many
places neere adioyning, to the impoueriſhing of many ſimple
people, as well Men as Women: Who were Arraigned and Conuiⅽted
for the ſame, at the Seſsions Houſe in the Old Bayly, the 14. of
Ianuarie, this preſent yeare, 1 6 1 3.

Printed at London for *Edward Marchant*, and are to be ſold at his ſhop
ouer againſt the Croſſe in Pauls Church-yard. 1 6 1 3.

5. As well as malefic witches, there existed a body of magical practitioners who
were generally thought to do good by the populace, but whose activities were
generally regarded with hostility by officialdom. This London couple were pilloried
in 1613 for various frauds perpetrated under the pretence of performing 'good'
magic and attempting to make contact with the spirit and fairy world (Bodleian
Library, University of Oxford, title page from 4°E17 Art(13)).

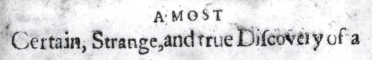

A MOST
Certain, Strange, and true Discovery of a
VVITCH.

Being taken by some of the Parliament Forces, as she was
standing on a small planck-board and saylit g on
it over the River of *Newbury*:

Together with the strange and true manner of her death, with
the propheticall words and speeches she vsed at the same time

✦✧✦✧✦✧✦✧✦✧✦✧✦✧✦✧✦✧✦✧ : ✦ : ✦✧✦✧✦✧✦✧✦✧✦✧✦✧✦✧✦

Pr nted by John Hammond, 1643.

6. Concern over and interest in witchcraft seems to have declined over the
1630s, but a by-product of the coming of the Civil Wars in 1642 was a renewed
interest in the subject. An early symptom of that interest was this pamphlet of
1643, describing the apprehension of a witch by parliamentary troops (Bodleian
Library, University of Oxford, title page from Douce WW 98).

7. The renewed concern over witchcraft was to result in 1645 in the mass trials of witches in East Anglia presided over by Matthew Hopkins, the 'Witch-Finder General'. This is the title page from Hopkins' defence of his witch-finding activities, showing the witch-hunter, two witches, and a selection of the familiars which figured so prominently in the Hopkins trials: Matthew Hopkins, *The Discovery of Witches: in Answer to severall Queries, lately delivered to the Judges of assize for the County of Norfolk* (London, 1647) (Author's collection).

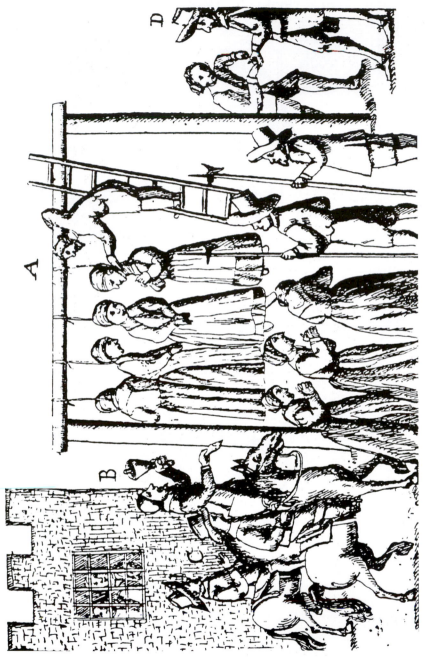

8. An outbreak of witch-hunting took place in Newcastle-upon-Tyne in the early 1650s, resulting in ten executions. This illustration depicts the execution of four of these witches. The incident was marked by the use by the city fathers of a Scottish witch-finder, who can be seen being paid at the right of the illustration. Ralph Gardiner, *England's Grievance discovered in relation to the Coal-Trade* (London, 1655) (Borthwick Institute of Historical Research, York).

9. Joseph Glanvill's *Saducismus Triumphatus*, first published under that title in 1681, was a major defence of belief in the spirit world in general and witchcraft in particular, was reprinted several times, and was to remain influential well into the eighteenth century. Here some of the phenomena whose reality is affirmed in the book are illustrated, among them, at right centre, the devil attending a witches' sabbat. Joseph Glanvill, *Saducismus Triumphatus; or full and plain Evidence concerning Witches and Apparitions* (London, 1681) (University of York Library).

10. Although witchcraft beliefs became marginalised among the educated, witch-craft continued to figure as a motif in elite culture. Here we have an early eighteenth-century depiction of MacBeth and the Weird Sisters, taken from an illustrated edition of Shakespeare's works first published in 1709, edited by Nicholas Rowe (University of York Library).

11. Witchcraft also continued to be a matter of recurring interest in popular culture, as demonstrated here by this crude woodcut illustrating a tract, first published *c.* 1750, describing the prophecies of Mother Shipton, the legendary witch from Knaresborough in Yorkshire. It is interesting that although reports of witches flying on broomsticks were almost totally absent from English witch-trials, the notion that they did so had clearly entered the popular imagination by the date of this woodcut. *The History of Mother Shipton* (University of York Library).

12. Another example of a witch on a broomstick, taken from William Hogarth's print of *c*. 1762 'Credulity, Superstition and Fanaticism'. The print, from which this is a detail, satirises several contemporary instances of imposture and delusion, and includes among the paraphernalia of superstition a book labelled 'Glanvill on Witches', and another labelled as 'Wesley's Sermons'. It is noteworthy that the image of the witch as an old lady with a sugar-loaf hat riding on a broomstick with her cat had already gelled by this date (University of York Library).

women normally formed only a very small proportion of those giving evidence in assize cases. Moreover, a further eighteen named women and an unspecified number of others were involved in searching for the witch's mark. This evidence should not be taken uncritically: it has been suggested that in many such cases women may have been giving evidence at their husband's instigation, while it has also been argued that all these women were simply stooges of patriarchy. But at first sight it would appear that this sample creates new avenues for investigating the link between women and witchcraft, and might well be worth exploring.

This suspicion is confirmed when we get deeper into this sample of cases, and find that at the centre of many of the accusations was concern over children [*Doc. 20*]. This finding is confirmed from materials from other areas, and it is clear that in the popular imagination children and adolescents were thought to have been particularly vulnerable to witch-craft, and this in a period when child care was regarded as an overwhel-mingly female activity. This finding possibly throws a new perspective on why it was so often middle-aged or elderly women who were accused: there are some powerful cultural forces at work in a model of witchcraft that has mothers accusing post-menopausal women of bewitching their children, a model which is redolent of points of conflict in the female age-structure. This has led to the proposal, based on Kleinian psychology, that the witch figure was essentially a refiguration of the bad mother [106]. Such proposals are speculative, but do demonstrate how the rethinking of witchcraft cases based upon a close reading of the documentation can lead in some unexpected directions. What is clear, however, is that the disputes which led to witchcraft often emerged in what the period would have regarded as female arenas of concern: child care, as we have noted, but also the defence against perceived infringements of domestic space and perceived disruptions of domestic order. Thus, for Dianne Purkiss, witchcraft beliefs enabled women to 'negotiate the fears and anxieties of housekeeping and motherhood', and she is correctly insistent that women's stories about witchcraft and witchcraft fears should be taken seriously by modern scholars [97 *p. 93*; cf. 127].

Some of these stories open up important insights into both popular mentalities and the individual circumstances which might lead a woman to confess that she was a witch. One such confession was given in 1647 towards the end of the Matthew Hopkins trials by Margaret Moore of Sutton in Cambridgeshire [113]. Moore's story told how three of her children had died, and that one evening she heard their voices calling for drink, and that she imagined the voice of her third child calling to her saying that if she did not give the child her soul it would take the life of her fourth, and only surviving, child. The voice of the dead child was, of course, really that of the devil, and Moore was sucked into a logic which, on her account, led her to enter the satanic pact, receive two familiars, and become a witch. What her tale indicates is how personal loss and psychological stress, coupled with the folklore of the period and the experience of living in an area where a witch-craze was flourishing, could lead an individual to think she was a witch. But it has been suggested that it is not just the psychological aspects of the early modern female experience which needs to be explored by students of witchcraft. It has also been argued (and here perhaps we confront the possibility of gaining a more sophisticated appreciation of the misogyny of the period) that there is a need to investigate contemporary attitudes to women's bodies. Dianne Purkiss, who has presented this case most clearly, has claimed that the witch 'reflected and reproduced a very specific fantasy about the female body in general and the maternal body in particular', suggesting that 'when understood in terms of the magic she performs and the power she exerts, the witch is a fantasy-image of the huge, controlling, scattered, polluted, leaky fantasy of the maternal body of the imaginary' [97 *p. 119*].

Future researchers into the connection between women and witchcraft will not, therefore, be short of perspectives upon their chosen topic: there is the nature of female power; the typology of the altercations between women which precipitated witchcraft accusations; the broader issues of attitudes to women, and perhaps more specifically post-menopausal women; the cultural elements upon which confessing witches drew when they constructed their confessions; and attitudes to the female body. However, to obtain a fully gendered impression of witchcraft we must not forget the presence of male witches. Frequently, male witches were the husbands or offspring of female witches, dragged in by association. But the Home Circuit indictments, to take one of the fullest available sources, show men being accused for independent acts of malefic witchcraft, and, intriguingly, for those broader forms of sorcery for which women were almost never indicted. There were three Surrey labourers who were indicted for using evil spells to help gain divers great sums of money in 1575; the man from West Ham in Essex indicted for invoking an evil spirit for the same purposes in 1576; and William Bennet from Finching-field in Essex who, it was alleged in 1588, had at various times and places invoked spirits to gain great sums of money, and by these means deceived and defrauded various of the queen's subjects [81 *pp. 131–2, 135, 162*]. Male witches, on the strength of these assize indictments, might be suspected of a wider range of occult activities than their female counterparts, and such cases remind us of that large proportion of cunning folk who were male. It would seem that when male and female witches are being contrasted, it is essential to be specific about exactly what form of occult activities they were suspected of.

This chapter has ranged widely and in it I have attempted to introduce not only a broad spectrum of early modern beliefs about witchcraft, but also suggest some of the main areas which as yet remain unexplored or contentious. Obviously, the constraints of writing briefly about many of the sometimes complicated issues involved has meant that large amounts of relevant material and interpretation have been compressed or omitted. I hope, however, to have left the reader with a clear impression of the richness and complexity of beliefs about witchcraft in early modern England, and also with some notion of the issues which are in need of further investigation.

5

The decline of witchcraft

In the 1630s, as we have seen, however tenacious witchcraft beliefs may have been among the population at large, witchcraft was becoming marginalised both as a matter of concern for central government and the criminal courts, and as a subject of intellectual and theological debate. No big demonological tracts were written, nor were any trial pamphlets, while on the strength of surviving documentation accusations of witchcraft were coming only very infrequently before both the secular and ecclesiastic courts, and when tried at the former were very unlikely to result in a capital conviction. Had the forces apparently at work in the 1630s been allowed to continue, historians of witchcraft in England might well have found little to concern them after that decade.

The Matthew Hopkins trials

But the Civil Wars came in 1642, and as an unforeseeable consequence witchcraft was re-established as a live issue. The most dramatic demonstration of this was furnished by the witch-trials which raged in eastern England between 1645 and 1647, and are associated with Matthew Hopkins, the Witch Finder General. The Hopkins episode has never been made the subject of a full-scale scholarly study, and in any case the fragmented and imperfect nature of the relevant sources [e.g., 14, 42] would probably render comprehensive research on the incident impossible. Yet even a brief account of what is currently known reveals that the history of the Hopkins trials is a remarkable one [80, 100 *chapter 5*]. In the winter of 1644–45 Matthew Hopkins, a gentleman living at Manningtree in Essex, became worried about what he perceived as the local prevalence of witches. His concerns apparently struck a responsive chord with a number of other people in the area, and led to the prosecution of 36 women, of whom about half were executed, at Chelmsford in July 1645. By this time witch accusations had spread into Suffolk, the county which saw the highest levels of prosecutions and executions, and there were also trials and hangings in Huntingdonshire, Norfolk, the Isle of Ely, and a number of counties in the east midlands, as well as several East Anglian borough towns. The imperfect nature of the records makes calculating an exact total of accused impossible, but an informed estimate would suggest that during this episode a minimum of 250 people were tried as witches or at least subjected to preliminary investigation, of whom a minimum of 100 (the real total may have been substantially over this) were executed. The Hopkins trials are of massive significance to the history of English witchcraft, not least because they offer a major challenge to those interpretations which would present witchcraft in England as a low key, non-demonic affair.

There was, even so, much about the content of these trials which was familiar. The overwhelming majority of those accused were poor and possibly elderly and marginalised women, and most of them appear to have been thought to have committed the usual types of *maleficium*. What was new was the widespread presence of the devil in the witches' confessions, with details of the pact and (more rarely, but with unusual frequency for England) accounts of sexual intercourse between the witch and the devil, although even in these confessions familiars appeared more frequently than did Satan [*Doc. 21*]. Much of this novel prominence of the devil may have been attributable to the interrogation techniques used by Hopkins and his associate, another obscure petty gentleman named John Stearne. These included, amidst more general maltreatment, sleep deprivation and use of leading questions. Explanations for the episode have perhaps tended to concentrate overmuch on the input of Hopkins and Stearne, but it is obvious that their witch-hunting activities, and the reputation they rapidly acquired for expertise in such matters, acted as a powerful catalyst.

But this catalyst acted within a distinctive context. Hopkins and Stearne both wrote tracts defending their actions [28, 41] [*Doc. 22*], and both were insistent that they only came to settlements to which they had been invited, or at which they knew they would be welcome. This may sound like special pleading, but there were certainly a number of elements present which made mass witch-trials a more likely prospect once the initial accusations had taken place. East Anglia was a parliamentarian stronghold, and although it had not seen serious fighting, the region was very much feeling the strains of warfare. The local administration was concerned with keeping the war effort going, and hence local justices of the peace who might otherwise have helped defuse witchcraft accusations at an early stage were preoccupied. Moreover, the ideological aspects of the war meant that in parliamentarian zones like East Anglia there was a shift towards a hard-line, more militant, and more popular Puritanism. Well-documented purges of clergymen thought to be ideologically un-reliable had taken place in both Essex and Suffolk, a leading role in exposing such clergy frequently being taken by just that class of yeoman farmer who so often acted as accusers in witchcraft cases. Moreover, in 1644 Suffolk had also seen an outbreak of officially-sanctioned icono-clasm, masterminded by a yeoman called William Dowsing, in the course of which, usually with the approval of Puritan onlookers, ornaments or stained glass in over a hundred parish churches had been smashed or defaced in an expression of extreme Protestant zeal. There was therefore just enough of a dilution of normal authority structures to permit witch-hunting to begin and to allow Matthew Hopkins to come to promin-ence, and a strong enough presence of popular Puritanism to allow a mass witch-hunt to develop from the initial accusations.

Hopkins, despite a pleasing legend that he was himself swum and executed as a witch, died of consumption in 1647, and John Stearne passed into obscurity a little later. There were to be no other episodes of witch-hunting to equal those over which they had presided, but the 1640s and 1650s were to witness a number of local outbreaks. The most severe came in Newcastle-upon-Tyne in 1650, when the town's Puritan administration called in a Scottish witch-pricker to help them hunt witches, with the result that 30 suspects were tried and fifteen executed [100 *p. 218*]. In Kent, a county which had previously experienced only a low level of accusations, there was a rise in trials with a local craze at Faversham in 1645, and clusters of indictments and executions at the assizes in 1652 and 1657 [82 *pp. 303–5, 321–2*, 81 *pp. 249–51*]. Cheshire, a county where witchcraft accusations had been very rare, saw a small upsurge of indictments in the 1650s, with separate groups each of three women being hanged in 1653 and 1656 [82 *pp. 418–19*]. To such trials was added a revival of publications about witchcraft. Trial pamphlets began to appear again, some of them very detailed [e.g., 32]. Some full-scale books were also published, among them sceptical works by John Gaule and Thomas Ady [21, 1], while Reginald Scot's *Discoverie of Witchcraft* was republished in 1656.

The post-Restoration situation

By the Restoration in 1660 witchcraft was therefore obviously back on the agenda on both a judicial and an intellectual level. Rather unexpectedly given the situation in the 1630s, it was to remain so for another three generations, effectively until the repeal of the witchcraft statutes in 1736. There was, as the last chapter demonstrated, a bedrock of popular beliefs which followed a different trajectory of change, but on an official and intellectual level it would seem that witchcraft in early modern England went through two phases. The first of these ran from the early 1560s until the 1630s, the second, initiated by the disruptions of the Civil Wars, from the 1640s until the early eighteenth century. Certainly in the England of 1660 witchcraft was a phenomenon about which a number of attitudes might be held. For many, the Civil War and Interregnum had marginalised witchcraft: witch-hunting was seen as symptomatic of an unhappy period when religious fanaticism reigned and when relatively obscure men like Matthew Hopkins could come to prominence. Hence both the conservatively-minded and sophisticated sceptics could write witch-hunting off as an activity characteristically indulged in by plebeian religious enthusiasts. Indeed, this attitude could derive ammunition from the way in which at least some nonconformists were able to claim that they maintained true religious values, among which was a tendency to take the works of the devil, and hence witchcraft, very seriously. But those anxious to establish an Anglican consensus in matters religious also found attitudes to witchcraft a matter for concern. Large-scale witch-hunts on the Hopkins model were clearly undesirable, redolent as they were of popular Puritanism. But the need to maintain witchcraft beliefs was seen as an element in keeping up the defences against new enemies, atheism and deism. If people ceased to believe in witches, they would next cease to believe in the devil, after which belief in the Christian God would go. Hence after 1660 attitudes to witchcraft as an intellectual or theological issue became increasingly enmeshed in the broader religious politics of the period.

Whatever else was happening with witchcraft in the post-Restoration period, the trials were continuing. Records from the Home Circuit of the assizes and from the Court of Great Sessions at Chester demonstrate this, while at this later date better record survival permits us to draw on evidence from a number of other areas. From 1658 gaol books, admittedly giving only very sparse details of trials, survive for the Oxford Circuit of the assizes, comprising the counties of Berkshire, Gloucestershire, Herefordshire, Monmouthshire, Oxfordshire, Shropshire, Staffordshire and Worcestershire [82 *pp. 435–9*]. From 1670 gaol books also survive for the Western Circuit, which comprehended Cornwall, Devon, Dorset, Somerset and Wiltshire [82 *pp. 439–46*]. Moreover, from the 1640s imperfect runs of indictments and depositions survive from the Northern Circuit, including Cumberland, Durham, Lancashire, Northumberland, Westmorland and Yorkshire [82 *pp. 393–7*]. Taken together these series of court materials suggest that witch-trials were probably running at what were, by English standards, fairly high levels in the 1650s, but that everywhere they declined quite sharply after 1660 and that this decline continued as the seventeenth century progressed. The last indictment at the Court of Great Sessions at Chester, levelled against a woman named Mary Baguley and unusual in that it resulted in a capital verdict, came in 1675 [82 *p. 422*]. The last indictment on the Oxford Circuit, resulting in the acquittal of a woman named Hannah Jarvis, came in 1689 [82 *p. 439*]. On the Western Circuit the last witchcraft indictment, involving a woman named Mary Stevens, came in 1707 [82 *p. 446*]. On the Home Circuit the last trial, of which we shall hear more later, came in 1712 and involved a woman named Jane Wenham [117].

The nature of the surviving records, especially the gaol books which sometimes give only the most skeletal information about trials, make it difficult to trace changes in the nature of prosecutions. What does seem clear, however, is that after the Restoration most accusations of witchcraft involved bewitching humans, most often to death. There were accusations of consorting with spirits, as when (to take a very late case) a widow and two labourer's wives were indicted at the Kent Summer Assizes in 1692 for consulting and covenanting with evil spirits in the shape of mice [81 *p. 263*], but trials involving the alleged bewitchment of animals, a regular feature of Elizabethan indictments, were very rare after 1660. We have seen how, in 1653, Sir Robert Filmer commented that judges generally only brought capital convictions for witchcraft when death of a human was allegedly involved, and this seems to have affected the nature of the formal accusations brought to the assizes. In any case, executions for witchcraft had become very rare. In Cheshire, as we have noted, the last such execution came in 1675. The last definitely known on the Home Circuit came somewhat earlier, when three women were hanged in Kent in 1657 [81 *p. 108*]. On the Oxford Circuit the last guilty verdict apparently came in 1664, although it is uncertain if the accused, a Staffordshire woman called Mary Denton, was actually executed [82 *p. 437*]. The last person known to have been sentenced to death, and in all probability hanged for witchcraft, was Alice Molland, condemned at Exeter in March 1685 [82 *p. 444*].

Exeter had, in fact, three years previously witnessed the condemnation and execution of three other women, Susanna Edwards, Mary Trembles and Temperance Lloyd, all of them from Bideford in Devon. This case is well documented [31, 43, 45], and is especially noteworthy for the full confessions given by the three women, all of whom told tales of meeting the devil. This is one of many English witchcraft cases which would repay deeper investigation. 1682 was a year in which Charles II's regime was taking a more aggressive line as the popular political activity unleashed by the Popish Plot receded, and it would be interesting to see if the accusations against the three women were in any way determined by the context of political or religious splits in Bideford or Devon more generally [*Doc. 23*]. What is obvious is that there was considerable popular odium against the suspected witches. This was noted in a subsequent commentary, which is generally accepted as concerning this incident, written at a later point by Roger North, a member of a prominent legal family, one of whose members had been in the courtroom at Exeter in 1682 [144, vol. 1 *pp. 168–9*, vol. 3 *pp. 130–1*]. North noted that the accused 'were brought to the assizes with as much noise and fury of the rabble against them as could be shewed on any occasion', and remarked that 'a less zeal in a city or kingdom hath been the overture of defection and revolution, and if these women had been acquitted, it was thought the country people would have committed some disorder'. The death sentence passed on the alleged witches was, according to North, largely the outcome of a weak judge caving in before this popular pressure.

Science

North's comments, with their mentions of the 'noise and fury of the rabble', and of 'defection and revolution', remind us of how witchcraft had now acquired political overtones: to this upper-class, legally-trained observer, popular wrath against witches had overtones of the popular political activity of the 1640s and 1650s, memories of which clearly had not dimmed in the subsequent decades. But by 1682, according to many accounts, there existed the stirrings of a new intellectual tendency which was to challenge witch beliefs, and render them even more clearly part of the mental world of the 'rabble'. This tendency was the bundle of intellectual changes which historians have termed the 'Scientific Revolution', a major shift in thinking whose apotheosis, for English historians at least, was attained in the life and works of Sir Isaac Newton (1642–1727). Certainly, in the later decades of the seventeenth century there existed a large amount of exciting, innovative, and sometimes fruitful thinking and speculation in that intellectual sphere which the period knew as natural philosophy. Various groups of scholars had been meeting together to discuss scientific matters in the 1640s and 1650s, and in 1662 they gained both a secure institutional base and recognition from the highest level when Charles II granted a charter to the Royal Society.

Knowledge of these intellectual developments has led to claims that new 'scientific' ways of thinking were in large measure responsible for displacing notions of witchcraft and magic, an important stage in that wider process by which the superstition and obscurantism of past ages was replaced by modern rationality. Such a view was of obvious appeal to post-Enlightenment Europeans who had a simplistic belief in progress and were also convinced that science was an ideologically innocent and unreservedly benevolent force. On a closer inspection, however, the relationship between the coming of the Scientific Revolution and the decline of magic and witchcraft seems more complex and a lot less certain than it might have appeared to nineteenth-century rationalists. Certainly, apologists for the belief in witchcraft who were writing in England in the late seventeenth and eighteenth centuries did not see new 'scientific' thinking or methods as their major problem. For such apologists the big problem was an overstated fear of atheism, of the possibility that Christianity might be threatened. Allied to atheism, they thought, was a spirit of mockery and drollery: there were fears that witchcraft beliefs, and with them possibly religious beliefs themselves, might be laughed out of existence by the shallow wits of the period. They saw the threat as coming from works like John Wagstaffe's *The Question of Witchcraft Debated* of 1669 rather than Newton's publications on optics.

Perhaps the most important point which has not been grasped in many later interpretations of the decline of witch beliefs is that scepticism about witchcraft had always been present, and that even when it became fashionable in the years around 1700 it was not total. Few people in those years, it would seem, were able to reject the idea of witchcraft totally. Far more common was an attitude which, while accepting the abstract possibility of witchcraft, was unable to accept that most stories about witchcraft, even those reconstructed into a formal accusation of witchcraft before an assize judge, were realistic. There had always been a strong streak, if not of scepticism, at least of caution in English attitudes to witchcraft. Demonologists were aware that witchcraft accusations might come from malice or popular superstition. The low conviction rates in English witch-trials suggest that assize judges were equally alert to these problems, while, as we have seen, some of the better-documented cases demonstrate that witchcraft accusations were often disputed in the very communities where alleged witches and their accusers lived. And there was also, it will be remembered, that theological strand, obviously accepted by some educated English Protestants, that most witchcraft beliefs sprang from ignorance of correct religion and a lack of Christian instruction, that the misfortunes so often attributed to the witch should in truth be ascribed to divine providence, and that to alot too much power to the witch and her master the Devil was merely to dishonour God. Any growth of 'scepticism' about witchcraft in the later seventeenth century was therefore able to build upon a well-established body of doubts on the subject. Witch beliefs, we must remind ourselves, were neither monolithic nor hegemonic.

This very plurality of beliefs about and intellectual positions on witchcraft theory made the task of post-Restoration Anglican writers on witchcraft all the more urgent, their fundamental problem being to construct a theory of witchcraft which would help serve as a bulwark against atheism but which would also avoid the encouragement of over-enthusiastic witch-hunting in the Matthew Hopkins mode. Although perhaps not in the Anglican mainstream, an important figure in this process was Henry More (1614–1687) [141]. As an undergraduate at Cambridge, More was influenced by the Christian Platonism which was then fashionable there. He was to remain interested, and at times immersed, in mystical theology until his death, but he was also very much in touch with the scientific developments of the period, and in particular studied the writings of Descartes in some depth. In 1653 he published an important defence of the spirit world in his *Antidote against Atheism*. More firmly in the Anglican mould was Meric Casaubon (1599–1671). Casaubon was a parish priest when the Civil Wars began and was deprived of his living by parliament in 1644, but returned as a Church of England minister after the Restoration. In 1670 he published *Of Credulity and Incredulity in Things Divine*, which argued for the existence of witchcraft and witches. A later contribution, appearing in 1684, was Richard Bovet's *Pandaemonium, or the Devil's Cloyster*. Bovet, a Somerset gentleman who had matriculated at Oxford in 1658, provided his readers with a number of detailed case studies relating to various occult phenomena, a technique which had in fact been firmly established by the most influential of this group of writers, Joseph Glanvill [*Doc. 24*].

Glanvill (1636–80) was born at Plymouth, entered Oxford in 1652, took his BA and MA, becoming influenced by Cambridge Platonism and an admirer of Henry More in the process. He subsequently became a minister in Essex, then held various livings in Somerset before attracting the attention of Charles II and becoming a Chaplain in Ordinary to the king in 1672. Throughout he maintained a keen interest in the scientific thinking of the period, and became a Fellow of the Royal Society in 1664. In 1666 he published *Some Philosophical Considerations touching Witches and Witchcraft*, the fourth edition of this being retitled *A Blow at Modern Sadducism* when it appeared in 1668. In 1681 an extended version of the work was republished under what was to become its final title, *Saducismus Triumphatus*, which could be rendered in English as 'Unbelief Overcome'. Glanvill's book demonstrated that at the time of its writing there was no necessary compartmentalisation between religion and science, while it is remarkable in using what the age would have regarded as scientific method in demonstrating the existence of witch-craft and of the spirit world more generally. The work enjoyed an endur-ing popularity: further editions came in 1689, 1700 and 1726, and it was to remain influential well into the eighteenth century.

As Glanvill demonstrates, 'science' in the late seventeenth century offered little ammunition for persons sceptical about the reality of witch-craft [126]. The rejection of occult and spiritual influences by natural philosophers was a longer and more difficult process than has often been supposed by triumphalist accounts of the onward march of science, rationality and progress, a point emphasised by Isaac Newton's keen interest in alchemy and in biblical prophecy, and by the acceptance of occult influences by that other leading scientific figure of the period, Sir Robert Boyle (1627–91). At best, there was a slow process taking place in which old ways of categorising and compartmentalising knowledge (this was essentially the polymathic age) were changing. The old system (perhaps demonstrated at its clearest in neoplatonism) of correspond-ences, of the interplay between the microcosm and the macrocosm, of sympathetic actions and hence sympathetic magic, was becoming less tenable. Newly located and more definite wedges were being driven between the scientific and the occult, between the natural and the spir-itual, and hence magic and witchcraft were becoming marginalised. New ideas on scientific method and scientific proof were doubtlessly aiding this process, although it should be noted that Joseph Glanvill was quite happy to regard the case histories of witchcraft and other occult phenomena he laid before his readers as matters of objective, 'scientific' fact.

Although many later writers on witchcraft were aware of the advances in knowledge and the onward march of natural philosophy in their period, few authors used them either as their main platform for attacking the belief in witchcraft, or as something to be attacked when the belief in witchcraft was being defended. The point is illustrated clearly by an important sceptical work published in 1677, John Webster's *The Displaying of Supposed Witchcraft*. Webster (1610–82) was a Yorkshireman who after a varied career as a clergyman, schoolmaster, and chaplain to parliamentary forces in the Civil War had settled as a medical practitioner at Clitheroe in Lancashire. His book drew on the medical and scientific knowledge of the day. But it was essentially written within a theological framework, depended heavily on Webster's interpretation of scripture, and had as its main objective not the complete denial of the supernatural in everyday life, but rather the denial of the devil's influence in the supernatural. Webster's main problem, like Glanvill's, was to define the balance of the natural and the supernatural worlds, and his conceptual framework was, for his contemporaries, therefore a very familiar one. The lack of impact of 'new' scientific thinking on works of scepticism was demonstrated even more tellingly by a tract appearing six decades after Webster's book, and in fact published in 1736, by coincidence the year in which the witchcraft statutes were repealed. It was the published version of a sermon preached by a Leicestershire clergyman named Joseph Juxon, who was dismayed when a witch was swum by his parishioners. The arguments he put forward were expressed in the measured tones of the early Enlightenment, but their content was essentially similar to that of the arguments against witchcraft which Reginald Scot had put forward a century and a half previously [*Docs 26 and 4*].

The last debate

Indeed, the last major work in defence of the belief in witchcraft, *The Compleat History of Magick, Sorcery and Witchcraft*, was written by a medical doctor, Richard Boulton (fl. 1697–1724), who was clearly in touch with some of the most advanced scientific and philosophical thought of the period. Most of his other writings were on medical matters, but he also published an epitome of Robert Boyle's works, while in his *Compleat History*, he was to refer approvingly to what was at the time an important and progressive work, John Locke's *Essay on Human Understanding* of 1690. Yet the main arguments Boulton was to put forward were what were by the early eighteenth century very familiar ones, his major contention being that the weight of evidence in favour of witchcraft was so great that it had to be accepted.

> the diabolical arts of witchcraft, sorcery, and the other magical performances, have been practised thro' so many ages, and in so many countries, with such dreadful and surprizing effects; and have been attested by the authority of testimony of so many writers of undoubted repute and credit, that it would be as absurd and unreasonable to deny the truth of such relations, as to dispute the existence of that diabolical power by which they were performed, or of those pernicious instruments the Devil makes use of to put them in practice. [4 *pp. 1–2*].

He argued that the swimming test and the identification of the witch's mark were important means of establishing proof in witchcraft cases. And he used in support of his views references to a number of case histories, ranging from the Warboys affair to the Salem trials of 1692.

Boulton's *Compleat History* was the spur to the publication of what is widely regarded as the last of the major English witchcraft texts, Francis Hutchinson's *An Historical Essay concerning Witchcraft*, which appeared in 1718 (it should be noted, however, that Boulton published a restatement of his views in 1722 [*Doc. 25*]). Hutchinson had been developing his ideas on witchcraft for some time, but had been persuaded at earlier points that publication on an issue which was contentious and politically loaded might not be to his advantage: he was a young churchman on the way up, and was eventually to become bishop of Down and Connor in 1721. When Hutchinson's work eventually appeared it was careful and scholarly, full of admiration for the Royal Society and the rationalism of recent developments in natural philosophy in England. It was based on a mass of information, being especially rich in evidence on the Matthew Hopkins affair. Hutchinson, however, demonstrated what was by then probably the mainstream 'sceptical position' by redefining what were acceptable and unacceptable views of the spirit world. 'The sober belief in spirits', he stated, was 'an essential part of every good Christian's faith', but such a belief was totally distinct from 'the fantastick doctrines that support the vulgar opinion of witchcraft' [29 *p. vi*]. His arguments in rejection of witch beliefs were as standard as Boulton's defence of witchcraft doctrine had been: most of what was attributed to witchcraft was, in fact, explicable in terms of natural causes; hostile references to witchcraft in Scripture were misunderstood or mistranslated; and the spectral evidence which had featured so prominently in seventeenth-century trials was patently a nonsense.

Hutchinson was clearly writing within a religious (and hence by extension political) framework which had moved on from that within which William Perkins had operated. The history of religion, and especially of Anglican thought, in the late Stuart and early Hanoverian periods is a complex subject, not least because of its entanglement with the constantly shifting politics of the period. But one theme which can, if at times uncertainly, be traced in the theological and religio-political debates of the late seventeenth and early eighteenth centuries was a gradual decline among the more educated Christians in the acceptance of divine providence as a force in the minutiae of everyday human affairs. The changing mood is probably most neatly symbolised by a related development, the general acceptance among advanced theologians that miracles were no longer operating as a proof of revealed religion. Educated people were still, overwhelmingly, devoutly Christian, and accepted the power of the Almighty to direct human affairs. But to seek the hand of God in all daily happenings, or to be too avid in tracing the Almighty's influence in such wonders as apparitions, floods, shipwrecks, monstrous births, and other anomalous or disastrous happenings was no longer acceptable among the educated, as, of course, was too literal a belief in the devil. By the early eighteenth century many Anglicans were well on the way to demonstrating that 'rational' Christianity which was to become a hallmark of the Enlightenment.

The decline of witch beliefs

The changing religious attitudes of the period serve to indicate broader attitudinal shifts. As we have suggested, an interpretation which sees the rejection of witchcraft among educated people purely in terms of the triumph of a rationalism founded on the impact of the Scientific Revolution doesn't really work. But as we have noted with both Hutchinson's major work and Juxon's published sermon, the reasons for rejecting belief in witchcraft being put forward in the early eighteenth century were very similar to those put forward by Reginald Scot 150 years earlier. The difference was that a majority of people were now willing to accept them. The mental world had changed. Yet it needs to be emphasised that, as far as can be seen at the present, it was essentially the mental world of the educated which had altered. The lower orders seem to have been happy to retain witch beliefs, although there are intriguing traces of a popular scepticism, evidence for which will never be more than very fragmentary. Consider, for example, a conversation in a Leeds alehouse in 1684, when discussion turned to Richard Marshall of nearby Horsforth, who, it was claimed, 'could cure men and horses that were bewitched by a charm'. Robert Speight, one of those drinking there at the time, commented that

> he knew Richard Marshall very well and that he was an ignorant fellow and could neither write nor read and that he was confident he was no witch, but as for his wife, she was as likely to be one as another, but he believed there was no witches. [146 p. 13]

The imputation that by 1684 you had to be literate to be taken seriously as a cunning man is intriguing, as is Speight's assertion that Marshall's wife could be a witch. But most interesting is Speight's belief that there 'was no witches': one is left wondering how many others among the lower orders shared this point of view.

Such changes as took place, despite such fascinating glimpses into plebeian notions about witches, are easier to trace among the educated. We have noted a number of such shifts, but perhaps the most fundamental, if the most elusive, was the transition from a view of the cosmos which saw it essentially as disordered to one which saw it as ordered and predictable. The world of the educated Englishman or woman of 1700, a world where the politics were explained by John Locke and the cosmology was explained by Isaac Newton, was obviously a fairly secure place: certainly educated commentators on the cosmos, society, and human nature seem to have sloughed off that essentially fraught and pessimistic tone which imbues so much writing on such topics in the years around 1600.

There were also more mundane forces at work. Throughout the period of the witch persecutions, demonologists and sceptical writers alike had been apt to comment adversely on popular superstitions and on the credulousness of the masses. John Cotta, the early seventeenth-century physician who wrote on the medical aspects of witchcraft, was typical in this respect. Like many educated observers he rejected the swimming test, arguing that it might offer the chance to hunt witches 'without allowance of any law, or respect of common civilitie' to 'every private, rash, and turbulent person, upon his own surmise of a witch'. Developing his theme, he continued:

> Though this kind of tryall of a witch, might haply prove it selfe worthy to be allowed, yet it is not in every private person iustifiable, or tolerable, or without warrant of authoritie in any sort excusable. The manner therefore of this vulgar tryall, must needs with iust and honest mindes, uncontroversedly, and undoubtedly, be rustical, barbarous and rude. [11 *p. 134*]

It was not, perhaps, a very big step from seeing over-enthusiastic practices on the fringes of witchcraft accusations as 'rustical, barbarous and rude' to regarding the whole of witch beliefs in that light.

This possibility became more open in the later seventeenth century. The decades around 1700 saw the firm establishment of a set of very definite ideas on the nature of 'polite' society, and of the desirability of joining it, a development which marked a growing cleavage between elite and popular culture. One aspect of this was a distancing of those who would consider themselves to be 'polite' from the belief in witchcraft, which was identified, at least as far as the generality of notions of what witches were meant to do, as 'vulgar'. Hence Roger North, commenting on the Exeter trials of 1682, could describe the confessions the condemned made on that occasion as 'mean and ignorant, and in the style of the vulgar tradition of sucking teats &c' [144, vol. 3 *p. 131*]. As we have seen, Francis Hutchinson, writing in 1718, could speak of 'the fantastick doctrines that support the vulgar opinion of witchcraft', and described such doctrines as the cultural property of the 'credulous multitude', while he also commented on how the common people 'will ever be ready to try their tricks, and swim the old women, and wonder at and magnify every unaccountable symptom and odd accident' [29 *pp. vii, viii*]. Thus it would seem that cultural distancing, on occasion amounting to downright snobbery, was a greater force in persuading polite society to reject witch-hunting than was the impact of rationalism.

One group of people who definitely rejected existing attitudes to witchcraft accusations, and hence to the beliefs which underlay them, were judges. As we have noted at several points, English assize judges had normally been cautious in their conduct of witch-trials, and this caution seems to have blossomed into a more thoroughgoing scepticism in the years following 1660. A well-known exception to this trend, of course, came in 1662, when that hero of the English Common Law tradition, Matthew Hale, presided over the trial of two witches, both of whom were convicted and executed, at Bury St Edmunds [47, 85]. Later in the century, however, the upper ranks of the judiciary seem to have been very reluctant to convict in witchcraft cases, perhaps the most significant figure here being Sir John Holt, another very well-regarded judge. In 1701 Holt tried Richard Hathaway, a youth who had a year previously indicted a woman called Sarah Moordike or Moorduck for bewitching him, and who now found himself on trial for false accusation. Holt subjected Hathaway and those who witnessed on his behalf to stringent cross-examination, and made heavy use of medical evidence in exposing the fraudulent nature of the symptoms of bewitchment which Hathaway had displayed [46]. Judicial scepticism was also clear in the last English witch-trial to end in a conviction, that involving a Hertfordshire woman called Jane Wenham, indicted in 1712 [9, 20, 117]. The presiding judge, Sir John Powell, showed scepticism throughout the proceedings, bullied prosecution witnesses, and secured a reprieve for Wenham after the jury had returned a verdict of guilty. In general, therefore, judges were extremely unconvinced by witchcraft accusations: yet it should be noted that accounts of both the Hathaway and Wenham cases demonstrate that whatever judges might think, witchcraft beliefs were still very much alive among local justices of the peace, parish clergy, and the population at large.

The Wenham case illustrates another point. For a brief period in the early eighteenth century, theories of witchcraft became enmeshed in the 'rage of party' of the period, with scepticism seen as a Whig characteristic, and the acceptance of the validity of witchcraft beliefs being associated with the High Anglican Churchmen who provided ideological ammunition for the Tories. Hence Francis Bragge, who published three pamphlets in favour of Jane Wenham's conviction, was a high churchman, while the last we hear of Jane Wenham was that a few years later she was living under the care, and on the estate, of a Whig magnate. In a recent analysis of the issue Ian Bostridge has demonstrated how witchcraft theory was very much alive in the early eighteenth century, and that it informed elites of the period about the nature of the divine order, reinforced various sets of opinions about the relationship between the secular and the spiritual worlds, and provided a useful and at times potent metaphor and motif in religious and political debates [76]. As we have noted, one way of understanding the growth of official concerns about witchcraft in sixteenth-century Europe was that the witch figure could be construed as a powerful enemy to the Christian Commonwealths which the governing classes were then bent on constructing. But by the early eighteenth century England was a society where politics were being organised increasingly according to the framework of a two-party system, while a major consequence of the mid-seventeenth-century upheavals was the emergence of a *de facto* religious pluralism. The old notion of a Christian Commonwealth, although something like it may have been conceived of at certain points by the Tories, was simply redundant, and a side-effect of this was that witch theory was also rendered redundant on this level. As Bostridge's work demonstrates, witchcraft theory had been useful as a symbolic marker of the boundaries of the sacral state by providing a common enemy against whom orthodox Christians could unite. After a brief flickering at the time of the Wenham controversy, this ideological aspect of witchcraft beliefs seems to have collapsed very quickly.

Yet it still took nearly a quarter of a century for the Witchcraft Acts to be repealed, and for the crime of witchcraft to disappear from the English statute books. The background was a revival of controversy in church matters during the 1730s, many of them associated with Edmund Gibson, bishop of London, who attempted to advance ecclesiastical influence. The Act of repeal, whose origins remain very difficult to establish, was probably a minor aspect of a mood among the Whigs, certainly in line with Walpole's wishes, to curb high-flying churchmen. The only speaker against the repeal was James Erskine, Lord Grange, who evidently saw the repeal of the Witchcraft Acts as a serious affront to correct religion. But Erskine's speech was greeted with laughter and scorn, and apparently ended his career as a serious politician [76 *pp. 184–5*]. Parliament and the social groups from which those sitting there were drawn was no longer willing to accept witch theories, and by the statute 9 Geo. II, cap. 5 the Elizabethan and Jacobean Acts were repealed, as was the Scottish Act of 1563. It was now impossible to prosecute witches in an English court of law. There was, however, one complication: those claiming to tell fortunes by witchcraft or magic, or to find lost and stolen goods by these means, practices by which, the Act noted, 'ignorant persons are frequently deluded and defrauded', could still be prosecuted. If they were convicted, they would suffer the same penalty which the old statutes had imposed for lesser forms of malefic witchcraft: a year's imprisonment punctuated by four periods of standing on the pillory on market days. Thus even if the concept of malefic witchcraft as a criminal offence had been abolished, cunning folk could still be prosecuted, albeit as frauds rather than as agents of the devil.

But, of course, witchcraft beliefs did not simply disappear in 1736. They obviously were no longer tenable, or at least fashionable, in their full form among the political elite and in polite society. But even there there was more ambivalence, and perhaps a greater willingness to retain belief in witchcraft, than previous historians have thought. Certainly, it is striking that educated observers remained cautious about dismissing in its entirety belief in witches, apparitions, and spirits [*Doc. 27*]. The most recent historian commenting on the matter has stressed that throughout the eighteenth century, English elite thinking on witchcraft was characterised by a diversity of opinion, while at the very least instances of witchcraft continued to generate considerable interest on this level [84 *pp. 100–6*]. We are, moreover, very much left to ponder how long such beliefs lingered, if only partially, among country justices of the peace and country clergy. As the eighteenth century progressed, belief in witches among such people may have declined terminally, but a lively interest in astrology reveals a continuing acceptance of the occult, an acceptance which was to surface again in the form of spiritualism in the nineteenth and early twentieth centuries, and in the current vogue for matters New Age.

Among the common people, as far as we can tell, witchcraft beliefs continued over the eighteenth century much as they had before. Certainly, when folklorists began their investigations in the nineteenth century they discovered that witch lore was widespread in the countryside, with beliefs in shape changing, in familiars, in the capacity of witches to harm people and animals through their malice, and in the powers of cunning folk [179]. Among countryfolk such beliefs, although becoming increasingly marginalised, survived into the twentieth century. They were finally banished by the spread of educated values, notably through universal education, and as a consequence of that final erosion of the small-scale societies where witch beliefs and fear of the witch had flourished. 'The popular belief in witchcraft', we are informed, 'declined largely because witchcraft was not adaptable to the fundamentally different uncertainties and demands of new market forces and modern mass culture' [79 p. 293]. The tenacity of such beliefs over the previous centuries demonstrates just how fundamental witchcraft has been to the human experience.

PART TWO

ASSESSMENT

6

Summing up

Our investigation into English witchcraft in the early modern period has revealed that it was a complex and multifaceted phenomenon which presents formidable challenges to the historical investigator, but which, these challenges notwithstanding, remains a fascinating and rewarding topic. At least part of its fascination is the way in which it shows how an historical problem can be investigated on a variety of levels and through a number of avenues. As I have tried to make clear, privileging any approach to the history of witchcraft runs the risk of over-simplification. Yet I would contend that the subject is best approached on three, albeit interconnected and interacting, levels. There is the one which, since the work of Alan Macfarlane and Keith Thomas, has been the most familiar, that represented by the sets of issues and type of evidence provided by the witch-trial, and by the build-up of community and interpersonal tensions which so often preceded it. To this must be added the problem of witchcraft as a matter of concern to our early modern forebears on an intellectual, theological, and (to use that modern term again) scientific level. Investigation of this problem has, as we have noted, recently been reopened. To this must be added a third theme, again one which was signposted by Macfarlane and Thomas: namely, how witchcraft and associated beliefs operated in the broader culture of early modern England. These three levels are not mutually exclusive and should be regarded, as I have suggested, as interconnected and interacting. But they do at least permit initial focal points which allow thoughts to be clarified and evidence to be assessed and organised before moving on to narrower or deeper matters.

Analysis of these different levels (and, indeed, any attempt to analyse early modern witchcraft) must be informed by a strict and well-informed contextualisation. This will help prevent the tendency so often demonstrated by modern observers who, in attempting to 'explain' what witchcraft was 'really' about, succeed merely in explaining away rather than offering a satisfying explanation. Above all, no modern investigator should lose sight of the fact that in the England of the period most people, from James VI and I to a villager seeking advice from local cunning folk on where to locate stolen goods, believed that the world was permeated with supernatural forces in a way that most denizens of the modern west do not. Witchcraft beliefs may have been fluid, variable, and contested, but they were inseparable from this overarching mental framework.

This fluid, variable and contested nature of early modern witchcraft beliefs should also make us very cautious about any monocausal interpretations of the witch-hunts. Above all, it is no longer possible to see the period of the witch persecutions in terms of any simplistic model of oppression or scapegoating. This model was established during the eighteenth-century Enlightenment, and received a tremendous boost in 1953 from *The Crucible*, Arthur Miller's successful dramatisation of the 1692 trials at Salem, Massachusetts, which is probably the most powerful influence on what educated people in the English-speaking world currently 'know' about witchcraft. In the large-scale witch-panics, like Salem in 1692 or in East Anglia in 1645, the normal restraints on witch-hunting broke down, and something like the witch-hunts of the modern imagination broke out. But more generally, in both England and New England, people had an informed and relatively sophisticated view of witchcraft, and, as we have seen, neighbours, local clergymen and local gentry might intervene on behalf of suspected witches, while, in England at least, the courts seemed surprisingly unwilling to bring convictions for witchcraft. In fact, recent rethinking on witch-trials in early modern Europe has presented the historian with a new and rather unexpected conundrum. The witch-craze, as we have noted, has frequently been connected to some of the major developments in late medieval and early modern Europe: the impact of the Reformation, the impact of the Counter-Reformation, the rise of the modern state, the arrival of rural capitalism and the concomitant break-up of the village community, and the all-pervasive misogyny of the period. These forces were operating, at a greater or lesser level, throughout Europe, yet the three centuries of witch-hunting which followed 1450 resulted in perhaps 40,000 executions. One of the biggest questions confronting the modern historian of witchcraft is, therefore, that of explaining why there were so *few* successful witch prosecutions in the early modern period.

One of the ways forward in the quest for gaining a deeper under-standing of early modern witchcraft, in England as elsewhere in Europe, is through the detailed case study. As we have noted, such studies have been carried out on the early seventeenth-century bewitchments of Mary Glover and Anne Gunter, on the Rye case of 1610 and the Lowestoft case which came to trial in 1662, while at least initial work has been com-pleted on the Warboys affair. A number of other well-documented cases await investigation. Carried out successfully, such case studies deepen our understanding through deepening our knowledge of the personalities and issues involved, through the uncovering of local enmities, faction struggles and power structures, and through the necessarily partial re-construction of how witch beliefs operated in all their subtlety and com-plexity. But amassing detailed local case studies will only prove useful if their importance is assessed on a comparative basis, and if the cumulative knowledge they will represent is subjected to that broader contextual-isation which has been alluded to.

There are, of course, a number of more focused themes which are in urgent need of deeper investigation. Perhaps the most important of these, as might have been deduced from the main text of this book, is the connection between women and witchcraft, or, more generally, the need to develop a fully gendered interpretation of witchcraft and witch beliefs. The connection between women and witchcraft is an issue which has attracted considerable attention, but despite the numerous publica-tions on the subject there is as yet only an imperfect and contested consensus about the nature of the main lines of debate. Other themes suggest themselves. For the historian of witchcraft in England, one of the most interesting but barely addressed phenomena connected with witchcraft is the witch's familiar. It seems that this was one of the great peculiarities of English witchcraft, yet the origins and significance of this phenomenon remain largely unexplored. Similarly, the medical aspects of witchcraft need further thought. The importance of cunning folk in giving advice when witchcraft was suspected is now widely recognised, but what might be termed official medical practitioners were also frequently involved, called upon by supposed victims of witchcraft or their parents, or asked to give expert evidence in court when trials took place [118, 129]. Witchcraft was thus a cause of concern to early modern doctors and physicians, and some, like John Cotta, John Webster and Richard Boulton, wrote books on the subject. A sensitive and informed reading of early modern materials by modern medical practitioners might also prove useful in opening up a possible understanding of what medical causes might have underlain the symptoms demonstrated in supposed cases of witchcraft or demonic possession.

Indeed, future investigation of early modern witchcraft in general will require the sensitive, informed, and deep reading of the relevant source materials which have come down to us, a reading whose underlying premise must be that what early modern people said and believed about witchcraft should be taken seriously. Attention to what was said reveals that although witchcraft, on any cultural level, was a malleable and unstable concept, it provided people with a way of thinking about and describing everyday events, with a language, with a discourse. This language, rooted in an acceptance of a magical universe which was shared between the accused witch and her accuser, allowed individuals to pursue interpersonal disputes, define personalities, and express emotions. Emotions, we must remember, were always very near the surface in witchcraft accusations, especially fear, hatred, and envy. To understand how these emotions operated in witchcraft cases, the historian must not only pay close attention to *what* was said, but also try to imagine *how* it was said, for so much in a witchcraft accusation revolved around speech and dialogue. The theoretical and methodological complexities for the historian of witchcraft seem capable of infinite expansion.

Having considered (or perhaps restated) some directions for future research we must now turn again to the refutation of a basic misconception. This book has been concerned with the history of witchcraft in England, yet even in a short work of this type the reader will have been aware of occasional references to, and comparisons with, the situation obtaining in Scotland and parts of continental Europe. As we have noted, there was a tradition that English witchcraft was somehow different from 'European' or 'continental' witchcraft. This view is no longer tenable. The best recent studies of witchcraft and witch-hunting in continental contexts [51, 53] demonstrate the existence of a range of problems which, albeit working themselves out in specific politico-religious and socio-economic contexts, generally look broadly comparable to those obtaining in Tudor and Stuart England. Witchcraft in early modern England, it must be reiterated, was a local version of the working out of a set of variables which were present throughout Europe, the essential factors being perhaps a relatively low-key Reformation and a relatively matured and centrally-controlled system for dealing with serious crime. One way of deepening our understanding of the situation in England, and in testing the importance of these or any other relevant factors, lies in the informed and sensitive application of a comparative approach involving other regional or national experiences of witchcraft, witch-hunting and witch beliefs.

Perhaps the final set of issues which needs to be restated here is that involved in the connections, if any, between witchcraft as it was under-stood, practised and persecuted in early modern England, and witchcraft as it is currently understood and practised among modern Wiccans and Pagans. Generally, despite claims made to the contrary, such connec-tions seem to be weak or non-existent. Even very sympathetic and sens-itive accounts of modern witchcraft demonstrate that it is very much an invented religion, a synthesis of magical beliefs (some adherents, of course, see this as a source of strength) which owes little to the witch beliefs of the late medieval and early modern periods [62, 66]. A more exciting prospect for historians of witchcraft in these periods is, perhaps, that opened up by the work of historians, folklorists and anthropologists on witchcraft and witch beliefs in nineteenth- and twentieth-century Europe. Work on France, for example, has demonstrated how witchcraft was one aspect of a richly documented system of popular beliefs in the nineteenth century [57], and how, in the *bocage* country of Normandy at least, witch beliefs, sometimes looking very like early modern ones, were still current in the 1960s [60]. There has been an important initial overview of post-1736 English witchcraft [79], but this has emphasised the need for more detailed work on this later period. Again, such studies will offer points of comparison to the historian of early modern English witchcraft, while even the current state of knowledge demonstrates some intriguing areas of continuity and change between early modern and later notions of witchcraft.

So, despite the numerous publications on the history of witchcraft, and more specifically English witchcraft, there still remains a lot of research to be done, a lot of questions which need to be better formulated, and a lot of better answers needed for those questions which we are confident have been more or less correctly posed. It is attractive to end with what is perhaps the biggest question of all. I, and I suspect most of my readers, do not believe in witchcraft and magic in the way in which, say, an Essex villager of around 1600 did. But most of our forebears did believe in something very like that, and even as I write, I suspect that a majority of the world's population still does so. This invites us to ponder on why it is that we inhabitants of an ever more technologically advanced, if ever more socially and ethically fragmented, west can do without such notions. Arguably, studying a little history might help illuminate this problem.

PART THREE

DOCUMENTS

Statute 5 Eliz. I, cap. 16, 'An Act against Conjurations, Inchantments and Witchcrafts' (English modernised). This is the text of this Act insofar as it concerns malefic witchcraft: there is a further section dealing with using magic to find treasure, etc.

Where at this present, there is no ordinary nor codign punishment provided against the practisers of the wicked offences of conjurations and invocations of evil spirits, and of sorceries, enchantments, charms and witchcrafts, the which offences by force of a statute made in the xxxiij year of the reign of the late King Henry the eighth were made to be felony, and so continued until the said statute was repealed by the Act and Statute of Repeal made in the first year of the reign of king Edward the vith; since the repeal whereof many fantastical and devilish persons have devised and practised invocations, and conjurations of evil and wicked spirits, and have used and practised witchcrafts, enchantments, charms and sorceries, to the destruction of the persons and goods of their neighbours and other subjects of this realm, and for other lewd intents and purposes contrary to the laws of Almighty God, to the peril of their own souls, and the great infamy and disquietness of this realm: for reformation whereof it be enacted by the Queen's Majesty with the assent of the Lords Spiritual and Temporal and the Commons in this present Parliament assembled, and by the authority of the same, that if any person or persons after the first day of June next coming, use, practise or exercise any invocations or conjurations of evil and wicked spirits, to or for any intent or purpose; or else if any person or persons after the said first day of June shall use, practise or exercise any witchcraft, enchantment, charm or sorcery, whereby any person shall happen to be killed or destroyed, that then as well every such offender or offenders in invocations or conjurations as is aforesaid, their counsellors & aiders, as also every such offender or offenders in witchcraft, enchantment, charm or sorcery whereby the death of any person does ensue, their aiders and counsellors, being of either of the said offences lawfully convicted and attainted, shall suffer pains of death as a felon or felons, and shall lose the privilege of benefit of clergy: saving the wife of such person her title or dower, and also the heir or successor of such person his or their titles of inheritance, succession and other rights, as though no such attainder of the ancestor or predecessor had been had or made.

And further be it enacted that by authority aforesaid, that if any person or persons, after the said first day of June next coming, shall use, practise or exercise any witchcraft, enchantment, charm or sorcery, whereby any person shall happen to be wasted, consumed or lamed in his or her body or member, or whereby any goods or cattles of such person shall be destroyed, wasted or impaired, then every such offender or offenders their counsellors and aiders, being thereof lawfully convicted, shall for his or their first offence or offences, suffer imprisonment by the space of one whole year, without bail or mainprise, and once in every quarter of the said year, shall in some market town, upon the market day or at such time as any fair shall be kept there, stand openly upon the pillory by the space of six hours, and there shall openly confess his or her error and offence; and for the second offence, being as is aforesaid lawfully convicted or attainted, shall suffer death as a felon, and shall lose the privilege of clergy and sanctuary: saving to the wife [*as above*].

> Statute 5 Eliz. I, cap. 16, 'An Act against Conjurations, Inchantments and
> Witchcrafts' (English modernised).

Document 2   WILLIAM PERKINS ON THE DEMONIC PACT

William Perkins (1558–1602) was the most celebrated English theologian of his day. His emphasis on the central importance of the demonic pact was widely shared among Protestant demonological writers of the period.

The ground of all the practices of witchcraft, is a league or covenant made betweene the witch and the devill: wherein they doe mutually bind themselves each to other. If any shall think it strange, that man or woman should enter league with satan, their utter enemie; they are to know it for a most evident and certen truth, that may not be called into question. . . . The ende why the devill seeketh to make a league with men, may be this; it is a point of his policie, not to be readie at every man's command to doe for him what he would, except he be sure of his reward; and no other meanes will serve his turne for taking assurance hereof, but this covenant. And why so? That hereby he may testifie both his hatred of God, and his malice against man. For since the time that he was come down from heaven, he hath hated God & his kingdome, and greatly maligned the happy estate of our first parents in paradise. For he thought to have brought upon them by their fall, eternal and finall confusion; but perceiving the covenant of grace, then manifested, and seeing man by it to be in a better and surere state than before, he much more maligned his estate, and beares the ranker hatred unto God for that his mercie bestowed upon him.

Now that he might show forth this hatred and malice, he takes upon him to imitate God, and to counterfeit his dealings with his Church. As God therefore hath made a covenant with his people, so satan ioynes in league with the world, labouring to bind some men unto him, that so if it were possible he might drawe them from the covenant of god and disgrace the same. Againe, as God hath his word and sacraments, the seales of his covenant unto his beleevers; so the devill hath his words and certaine outward signes to ratifie the same to his instruments.

> William Perkins, *A Discourse of the Damned Art of Witchcraft.*
> *So farre forth as it is revealed in the Scriptures, and manifest*
> *by true Experience* (Cambridge, 1608), pp. 41, 45–7.

DOCUMENT 3   WILLIAM PERKINS ON CUNNING FOLK

This is an unusually cogent statement of the view widely held among Protestant theologians that 'good' witches drew their powers from the devil as certainly as did the wicked ones, and should suffer accordingly. Perkins's comments on the popularity of cunning folk were also widely echoed by the writers of the period.

The healing and harmlesse witch must die by this law, though he kill not, onely for covenant made with Satan. For this must alwaies be remembered, as a conclusion, that by witches we understand not those onely which kill and torment; but all diviners, charmers, iuglers, all wizzards, commonly called wise men and wise women; yea, whosoever doe any thing (knowing what they doe) which cannot be effected by nature or art; and in the same number we reckon all good witches, which doe no hurt but good, which doe not spoile and destroy, but save and deliver. All these come under this sentence of *Moses*, because they deny God, and are confederates with Satan. By the lawes of England, the thiefe is executed for stealing, and me thinke it iust and profitable; but it were a thousand times better for the land, if all witches, but specially the blessing witch might suffer death. For the thiefe by his stealing, and the hurtful inchanter by charming, bring hinderance and hurt to the bodies and goods of men; but these are the right hand of the devill, by which he taketh and destroyeth the soules of men. Men doe commonly hate and spit at the damifying sorcerer, as unworthie to live among them; whereas the other is so deare unto them, that they hold themselves and their countrey blessed that have him among them, they flie unto him in necessitie, they depend upon him as their god, and by this meanes, thousands are carried away to their finall confusion. Death therefore is the iust and deserved portion of the good witch.

Perkins, ibid., pp. 255–7.

DOCUMENT 4   REGINALD SCOT ON DIVINE POWER

Reginald Scot's tract of 1584 was unrelentingly sceptical about the powers of witches, but a major theme informing the scepticism was a theological position which argued that the misfortunes popularly attributed to witches are in fact the result of God's power. Here he refutes those who overestimate the power of the devil and of witches.

. . . these make the divell a whole god, to create things of nothing, to knowe men's cogitations, and to doo that which God never did; as to transubstantiate men into beasts, &c. Which thing if divels could doo, yet followeth it not, that witches have such power. But if all the divels in hell were dead, and all the witches in England burnt or hanged; I warrant you we should not faile to have raine, haile and tempests, as now we have; according to the appointment and will of God, and according to the constitution of the elements, and the course of the planets, wherein God hath set a perfect and perpetuall order.

I am also well assured, that if all the old women in the world were witches; and all the priests [i.e., Roman Catholic priests], conjurers; we should not have a drop of raine, nor a blast of wind the more or lesse for them. For the Lord hath bound the waters in the clouds, and hath set bounds about the waters, untill the daie and night come to an end; yea it is God that raiseth the winds and stilleth them: and he saieth to the raine and snowe; Be upon the earth, and it falleth. The wind of the Lord, and not the wind of witches, shall destroie the treasures of their pleasant vessels, and drie up the fountaines; saieth *Oseias*. Let us also learne and confesse with the Prophet *David*, that we ourselves are the causes of our afflictions; and not exclaime upon witches, when we should call upon God for mercie.

Reginald Scot, *The Discoverie of Witchcraft* (London, 1584), book 1, ch. 1.

DOCUMENT 5   WITCHES AND ENTERTAINMENT AT COURT, 1609

Ben Jonson (?1573–1637) was one of the leading playwrights and poets of his day, and also turned his hand to writing masques, entertainments for the court of James VI and I and his queen, Anne of Denmark. The antimasque to his 'Masque of Queens' of 1609 consisted of a presentation of a group of witches to represent 'the opposites to good fame', good fame being the theme of the masque proper. Jonson left detailed instructions on the staging of this antimasque, and referenced his sources, demonstrating his knowledge of both current demonological works and classical allusions to witchcraft. The first extract describes the initial scene witnessed by the audience, the second describes the 'dame', or chief of the witches.

. . . the part of the scene which first presented it selfe, was a very ugly Hell: which flaming beneath, smoked unto the top of the roofe. And in respect all evills are, morally, said to come from Hell; as also from the observation of Torrentius upon Horace his Canidia, 'quae tot instructa venenis, ex Orci faucibus profecta videri possit' [one can see as many companies of witches as there are exits from hell]: These witches, with a kind of hollow and infernall musique, came forth from thence. First one, then two, and three, and more, till their number increased to eleven; all differently attyr'd: some with rats on their head; some on their shoulders; others with ointment pots at their girdles; all with spindles, timbrels, rattles, or other veneficall instruments, making a confused noyse, with strange gestures. The device of their attire was Master Jones [i.e., Inigo Jones] his, with the invention, of the whole scene, and machine. Onely, I prescrib'd them their properties of vipers, snakes, bones, herbs, rootes, and other ensignes of their magic, out of the authoritie of ancient and late writers . . .

The *Dame enter'd to them, naked arm'd, bare-footed, her frock tuck'd, her hayre knotted, and folded with vipers; in her hand a torch made of a dead man's arm, lighted; girded with a snake. To whom they all [i.e., the other witches] did reverence, and shee spake, uttering, by way of question, the end wherefore they came: which if it had beene done either before, or otherwise, had not beene so naturall.

*This Dame I make to beare the person of Ate, or mischiefe (for so I interpret it) out of Homer's description of her, *Iliad*, I, wher he makes her swift to hurt mankind, strong, and sound of her feet, and *Iliad*, T [sic] walking upright on men's heads, in both places using one, and the same phrase to signifie her power . . . I present her bare footed, and her frock tuck'd, to make her seeme more expedite, by Horace his authoritie, *Sat. 8. Lib. 1.* . . . But for her hayre, I rather respecte another place of his, *Epod. Lib. Ode. 5.* . . . And that of Lucan, *Lib. 6* speaking of Erithco's attire. . . . For her torch, see Remig. [i.e., Remigius, or Nicholas Remy, a French demonologist], *Lib. 2 cap. 3.*

Ben Jonson, The Workes of Beniamin Jonson (1616), pp. 945–6, 948.

DOCUMENT 6   REGINALD SCOT ON THE DYNAMICS OF WITCHCRAFT ACCUSATIONS, 1584

Here Scot provides us with a classic description of the 'charity refused' model of witchcraft accusations.

One sort of such as are said to bee witches, are women which be commonly old, lame, bleare-eied, pale, fowle and full of wrinkels; poore, sullen, superstitious, and papist; or such as knowe no religion: in whose drousie minds the divell hath gotten a fine seat; so as, what mischeefe, mischance, calamatie, or slaughter is brought to passe, they are easily persuaded the same is doone by themselves; imprinting in their minds an earnest and constant imagination hereof. They are leane and deformed, shewing melancholie in their faces, to the horror of all that see them. They are doting, scolds, mad, divelish: and not much differing from them that are thought to be possessed with spirits; so firme and stedfast in their opinions, as whosoever shall onelie have respect to the constancie of their words uttered, would easily believe they were true indeed.

These miserable wretches are odious unto all their neighbors, and so feared, as few dare offend them, or denie them anie thing they aske: whereby they take upon them; yea, and sometimes thinke, that they can doo such things as are beyond the abilitie of humane nature. These go from house to house, and from doore to doore for a pot full of milke, yea, drinke, pottage, or some such releefe; without the which they could hardlie live: neither obtaining for their service and paines, nor by their art, nor yet at the divels hands (with whom they are said to make a perfect and visible bargaine) either beautie, monie, promotion, welth, worship, pleasure, honor, knowledge, learning, or anie other benefit whatsoever.

It falleth out many times, that neither their necessities, nor their expectation is answered or served, in those place where they beg or borrowe; but rather their lewdnesse is by their neighbours reprooved. And further, in tract of time the witch waxeth odious and tedious to her neighbors; and they againe are despised and despited of hir: so as sometimes she cursseth one, and sometimes another; and that from the maister of the house, his wife, children, cattell, &c. to the little pig that lieth in the stie. Thus in processe of time they have all displeased her, and she hath wished evill lucke unto them all: perhaps with cursses and imprecations made in forme. Doubtlesse (at length) some of hir neighbors die, or fall sicke; or some of their children are visited with diseases that vex them strangelie: as apoplexies, epilepsies, convulsions, hot fevers, wormes, &c. Which by ignorant parents are supposed to be the vengeance of witches. Yea, and their opinions and conceits are confirmed and maintained by unskilfull physicians: according to the common saieng, *Inscitiae pallium maleficium & incantio*, Witchcraft and inchantment is the cloke of ignorance: whereas indeed evill humors & not strange words, witches, or spirits are the causes of such diseases. Also some of their cattell perish, either by disease or mischance. Then they, upon whom such adversities fall, weighing the fame that goeth upon this woman (hir words, displeasure, and cursses meeting so justlie with their misfortune) doo not onelie conceive, but also are resolved, that all their mishaps are brought to passe by hir onelie meanes.

Scot, *Discoverie of Witchcraft*, book I, ch. 3.

DOCUMENT 7 SOME EARLY DEPOSITIONS, ESSEX 1563

These were taken by the Archdeaconry courts, although Elizabeth Lowyes was tried shortly afterwards at the assizes. There she became the first person known to have been convicted under the 1563 statute. The evidence given here makes an interesting comparison to Scot's statements in the preceding extract.

Evidence of Philippa Geale [Gale], aged thirty-two, of Great Waltham: That Elizabeth Lewys, wife of John Lowys, and this depo[nen]t fell at varia[ti]ons for takynge in of worke, in that the said Lewys wif went to John Barnard's wif and said that this depo[nen]t wolld spyn no more of her worke. Thereuppon at the next meatynge they fell out. And this depo[nen]t tollde her that she lied and had tollde a wrong tale. And, amonge other talke, this deponent saiethe that she said 'Yf it be as folke saye, thow art a wytche'. To whome the said Lewys wif aunswered, 'Yf I be a wyche the dyvell thee twytche'. And ymmediatly upon that this depo[nen]t fell on a grete quyvering and quakeringe. And this was don about Satirday aboutes five yeres past. And soo after that [she] went home, continuynge soo till wednesdaie, at w[hi]ch daie she fell downe ded, and was so sick fourteen daies yt no bodie thought shee wolld have lyved. And then her neighbors sent for the preistes, to whom she utterid all. And then he sent for the said Lewys wif, threatenynge her if this depo[nen]t died she shulld be brent [i.e., burnt], and after her comynge this depon[nen]t mended.

And otherwise she knows nothing.

Agnes Devenyshe, aged forty-seven, of Great Waltham, where she had lived for eight years:

She hath herde a comon brute [i.e., rumour] that Lewys wife ys a witche. Item, that about M[ar]ch last, gooinge to Comes house, she wente to the said Lowys wiffes hous, and then they talked about a sore arme of hers. And then she [i.e., Lowys] counselled her to goo to a woman under Munckwoode. And goynge thith[e]r, the folkes told her husbande and her that she was a wytche.

It[em]. The saide Lewys wif did then and there aske her how Johnson drink did worke. And she this deponent aunswerid that yt was as yt did. Then the said Lewys wife said, 'Lett hym com and speke w[i]th me'.

It[em]. That this depo[nen]t goynge for her monnye, viz. vis viiid whiche she collde not spare, and aft[e]r that she had two piges and one of them sodenlie died, and the other ev[er] pyned till she was fayne to sell yt. And she judgeth that yt is the doinge of the said Lowys wiff. And then she this depo[nen]t fell sicke, w[i]th her husband and child w[i]thall, in pain and grief.

Item. That on Maye Even, being at Canell[es] hous, John Canell his chillde being sicke, laye w[i]th the neck clene awrye, the face und[er] the lift [i.e., left] shollder, and the right arme drawen w[i]th the hande clene backwarde and upwarde, the shullder pynt [i.e., point] before the brest pight, the bodie lyinge from yt an oth[er] waie, not right but wrythinge, and the right legge clene backwarde behinde the bodie, contrarie to all nature; as they suppose the verye doinge of the said Lowys wif.

And otherwise she knows nothing to depose.

Essex Record Office, at end of Archdeaconry of Essex Act Book, ERO, D/AEA/2.

DOCUMENT 8   ASSIZE INDICTMENTS FOR WITCHCRAFT, 1574

This is a fairly typical sample of indictments from the Elizabethan period (abstracted from the Latin originals) from the Summer Assizes in Essex held at Brentwood, 19 July 1574. Another woman, Cecily Glasenberye of Barking, was sentenced to death after being convicted on five counts of witchcraft at this assize. Sad to relate, further documentation reveals that Alice Hynckson died in prison of the plague in May 1575, about ten weeks before completing her sentence.

Elizabeth Taylor, wife of John Taylor of Thaxted, labourer, on 10 April 1573 at Thaxted bewitched Alice Holmes, daughter of William Holmes of London, basket-maker, who languished until 14 April following, when she died at Thaxted.

Pleaded not guilty: judged [i.e. found guilty and sentenced to death under the 1563 statute]

The same, on 10 October 1573 at Thaxted bewitched Agnes Townesend, daughter of William Townesend of Thaxted, carpenter, who languished until 20 May following, when she died at Thaxted.

Pleaded not guilty: judged

Alice Hynckson of Thaxted, widow, on 20 January 1572 at Thaxted bewitched three cows valued at £4, and seven ewes valued at 20 shillings, the goods and chattels of James Jarvys of Thaxted, husbandman, which died within four days.

Pleaded not guilty: guilty: sentenced to a year's imprisonment and four sessions on the pillory

Agnes Dix, wife of John Dix of Walter Belchamp, labourer, on 1 May 1574 at Walter Belchamp bewitched Richard Hayward, who languished for fourteen days subsequently.

Pleaded not guilty: not guilty

The same, on 20 January 1574 at Walter Belchamp bewitched Elizabeth Potter, wife of John Potter of Walter Belchamp, who languished until 30 January following, when she died at Walter Belchamp.

Pleaded not guilty: not guilty

Public Record Office, London, Clerks of Assize Records, Home Circuit Indictments,
PRO ASSI 35/16/4/14–15; 35/16/4/16: 35/16/4/22–23.

Document 9 WHY SO MANY WITCHES ARE WOMEN, 1616

Alexander Roberts was an obscure clergyman whose tract of 1616 consisted of a brief exposition of demonological theory, together with an account of the trial of a witch at King's Lynn appended. His explanations of why women were attracted to witchcraft are totally conventional for the period.

First, they are by nature credulous, wanting experience, and therefore more easily deceived.

Secondly, they harbour in their breast a curious and inquisitive desire to know such things as be not fitting and convenient, and so are oftentimes intangled with the bare show and visard of goodnesse . . .

Thirdly, their complection [i.e. psychological condition] is softer, and from hence more easily receive the impressions offered by the divell; as when they be instructed and governed by good angels, they prove exceeding religious, and extraordinary devout: so consenting to the suggestions of evil spirits, becoming notoriously wicked, so that there is no mischiefe above that of a woman, *Eccles*. 25.13.&c.

Fourthly, in them is a greater facility to fall, and therefore the divell at the first tooke advantage, and set upon Eve in Adam's absence, *Genesis* 3.3.

Fifthly, this sex, when it conceiveth wrath or hatred against any, is unplacable, possessed with unsatiable desire of revenge, and transported with appetite to right (as they thinke) the wrongs offered unto them: and when their power herein answereth not their will, and are meditating with themselves how to effect their mischievous proiects and designes, the divell taketh the occasion, who knoweth in what manner to content exulcerated mindes, windeth himselfe into their hearts, offereth to teach them the meanes by which they may bring to pass that rancor which was nourished in their breasts, and offereth his helpe and furtherance herein.

Sixthly, they are of a slippery tongue, and full of words: and therefore if they know any such wicked practices, are not able to hold them, but communicate the same with their husbands, children, consorts, and inward acquaintance; who not considerately weighing what the issue and end thereof may be, entertaine the same, and so the poyson is dispersed.

Alexander Roberts, *A Treatise of Witchcraft: wherein sundry Propositions are laid downe, plainely discovering the Wickednesse of that damnable Art* (1616), pp. 42–3.

DOCUMENT 10 WITCHES IN WEST YORKSHIRE, *c.* 1620

The Yorkshire gentleman Edward Fairfax began his account of his daughters' bewitchment with a description of the women he thought responsible. The list is typical, describing women of a generally bad character with an existing reputation for witchcraft. Note how familiars were by this date a core aspect of witchcraft beliefs, and also how Elizabeth Fletcher's reputation for witchcraft evidently worked to her advantage.

The women questioned for this offence are in number six, of whom five fall in my knowledge; therefore I can give you some character of them; and the spirits also I will describe, as the children demonstrated their shapes. The first is called Margaret Waite, a widow that some years ago came to dwell in these parts, with a husband; who brought with them an evil report for witchcraft and theft; the man died by the hand of the executioner for stealing, and his relict hath increased the report she brought with her for witcherie. Her familiar spirit is a deformed thing with many feet, black of colour, rough with hair, the bigness of a cat, the name of it unknown. The next is her daughter, a young woman, agreeing with her mother in name and conditions, and is thought, she added impudency and lewd behaviour; for she is young and not deformed; and their house is holden for a receptacle for some of the worst sort – her spirit, a white cat spotted with black, and named Inges.

The third is Jennit Dibble, a very old widow, reputed a witch for many years; and constant report confirmeth that her mother, two aunts, two sisters, her husband and some of her children, have long been esteemed witches, for that it seemeth hereditary to her family; – her spirit is in the shape of a great black cat called Gibbe, which hath attended her now above 40 years.

They are made up a mass by Margaret Thorpe, daughter of Jennit Dibble, lately a widow, for which she beareth some blame. This woman, if you read the sequel, will perhaps seem unto you, not without great reason, to be an obedient child and docile scholar of so skilful a parent. Her familiar is in the shape of a bird, yellow of colour, about the bigness of a crow – the name of it is Tewhit.

The fifth is Elizabeth Fletcher, wife of Thomas Fletcher, daughter to one Grace Foster, dead long since: a woman notoriously famed for a witch, who had so powerful hand over the wealthiest neighbours about her, that none of them refused to do anything she required; yea, unbesought they provided her with fire, and meat from their own tables; and did what else they thought would please her.

The sixth is Elizabeth Dickenson, wife of William Dickenson, of whom I cannot say much of certain knowledge; neither is her spirit known to us.

> *Daemonologia: a Discourse on Witchcraft as it was acted in the Family of Mr. Edward Fairfax, of Fuyston, in the County of York, in the Year 1621*, ed. William Grainge (Harrogate, 1882), pp. 32–4.

DOCUMENT 11 A CHURCH COURT DEFAMATION CASE, 1617

One reaction to accusations of witchcraft was to sue the accusers for defamation. A number of such cases survive in church court records, this one coming from the Leeds area. Note the public altercation between Thomas Brooke and John Beamond, the way in which witchcraft was gossiped about, Brooke's long-standing suspicions that Beamond was harming his cattle, and Ann Snowden's refusal to believe that Isabel Beamond was a witch. Other documentation for this case suggests that Beamond had been examined by local justices and committed to prison at York on suspicion of witchcraft a few days previously, although we have no evidence on the outcome of those proceedings or of this defamation suit. The statements reproduced here were taken on 28 November 1617.

Evidence of George Eastburne of Headingly in the parish of Leeds [Latin heading says Eastburne is aged about 50, has known Isabel Beamond well for about 30 years, and Thomas Brooke for about 34 years]:

Upon Sonday next after May Day last past he the ar[ticula]te [i.e., aforesaid] Thomas Brooke being in the towne gate or street of Burley situate within the p[ar]ishe of Leedes ar[ticula]te did goe unto the dore of the house of John Beamond, husband of the ar[ticula]te Isabell Beamond, and willed him the said John to come forth of the house into the said streete & threatened to fight w[i]th him, whereupon he the said John Beamond spooke unto the said Thomas Brooke through a windowe of his said house and tould him that he had three sonnes the worst of w[hi]ch would answere him. And thereupon the said Thomas Brooke tould the said John Beamond that both he & his wife were witches (meaninge she the ar[ticula]te Isabel Beamond), & further said that the said Isabell Beamond had bewiched his goodes & had been a wich for fortene yeres last of his knowledge: then & there being p[re]sent and hearinge the same wordes he this exa[mina]te, Henrie Moore, William Stevenson and divers others . . .

Evidence of Ann Snowden of Bramley in the parish of Leeds [Latin heading says Snowden is aged 21, has known both Isabel Beamond and Thomas Brookes for about seven years]:

That in May now last past as she certeynely remembreth, she this ex[amina]te being then a servant to one Edward Haigh in Burley w[i]thin the p[ar]ishe of Leedes ar[ticula]te was goeing into the towne fieldes of Burley to fetch her master's kine at w[hi]ch tyme & place the ar[ticula]te Thomas Brooke did ov[er]take this ex[amina]te in the said feildes & after some other speeches he tould this ex[amina]te that his kyne would give no milke, 'For I thinke', quoth he, 'that Isabell Beamond ar[ticula]te hath bewiched them (meaning the ar[ticula]te Isabell Beamond)', where-upon the ex[amina]te tould him that she thought the said Isabell was an honest woman. 'Ney', quoth he, 'she is a wich [meaninge the ar[ticula]te Isabell Beamond] & hath done me harme in my goods these xiiii yeares last past': then & there being p[re]sent this ex[amina]te & none other.

Borthwick Institute of Historical Research, York, Cause Papers, C.P.H2177.

DOCUMENT 12   COMMUNITY REACTIONS TO WITCHES, *c.* 1720

These are two extracts from Quarter Sessions records showing how community reactions to supposed witches could vary. The second extract (which is slightly damaged in the original) suggests a considerable cleavage between the attitude of the justices of the peace and that of the witch's community. The relatively late date of both these extracts is of some interest.

West Riding Com Ebor. To the Hon[o]rable the Justices of Peace at Barnsley Assembled.

Wee the inhabitants of Knottingley within the said Riding do hereby certify yo[u]r worships, that William Sefton yo[u]r compl[ain]ant is a man of a quiet disposistion frequenting the church & bringing his children up in the feare of God giveing them as good education as any person of his ability within us doth. But being dayly abused & threatened by one W[illia]m Howitt & Isabell his wife, by terming him a wizzard, I was forced to gett a warr[an]t against them from Esq. Harman who comitted them & sent them to ye house of correction, to which place S[i]r Rowland Winn had some yeares since sent them upon yo[u]r complainant's account had he not out of compastion to them put up the same. But being not able any longer to abide their reproaches was forced to doe what he hath & humbly desires that the s[ai]d Howitt may be dealt with as yo[u]r worships may see fitt, for that yo[u]r compl[ain]ant may live at quietness he being no such person as the s[ai]d Howitt terms him to be, to the best of our knowledge, is the request of yo[u]r worshipp's humble serv[an]ts. (Followed by 17 signatures)

West Yorkshire Record Office, Wakefield,
Quarter Session Rolls, QS1/62/10/ File 7: 1723.

To the overseer of the poor for the town of Hainsworth [Hainworth]. Whereas Ann Jackson of y[ou]r town hath been falsly & malitiously defam'd for a witch & that scandall hath been so industriously promoted by wicked people that all her neighbours refuse and avoid to have any dealing or com[m]erce with the s[ai]d Ann and she being thereby deprived of necessary sustenance & her former allowance of twelve pence being insufficient thereby for her maintenance, these are therefore to reqire & order you the overseer to allow & pay the s[ai]d Ann Jackson the sum of two shillings & six pence weekly & every week untill you shall have cause to the contrary. Hereof faile not at y[ou]r perill. Given under my hand . . . the 19th day of May in the year of our Lord 1719.

Joshua Bootham overseer of the poor of Hainsworth having this day appeared before us to appeal ag[ains]t the above written ord[e]r we think fitt to confirm it . . .

John Fountayne
Rob. Monckton

West Yorkshire Record Office, Wakefield,
Quarter Sessions Rolls, QS1/60/4/File 8: 1719.

DOCUMENT 13   THE GODLY REJECT COUNTER MAGIC, 1683

Here a worried parent consults two nonconformist ministers about how to treat her supposedly bewitched son. Note the description of the symptoms of bewitchment, the evident acceptance by the doctor of the efficacy of counter magic, and the recipe for the 'witch's cake': as the document notes, the idea was that burning the cake, by sympathetic magic, would inflict unbearable pain in the urinary tract of the bewitcher, who would then reveal herself when she came to investigate the cause of her torments. Oliver Heywood (1630– 1702) was a prominent West Yorkshire nonconformist minister, and his papers contain several references to witchcraft and related matters.

Came to my house – Judith Higson, and because I was not at home she writ down her business and left it for me, which was to desire my advice in a weighty case, she had also gone to Mr Dawson's, but found him not at home, the case was this. She hath a sone by her former husband Abraham Swift (called also Abraham) who hath lyen long under a strange and sad hand of God in his body; he lyes in bed, hath swelling in his throat, hand, cannot stirre, looks as one affrighted, about 12 years of age – they had used many meanes for his cure, but all inefficient, that day, May 7, came to their house (not sent for by them but brought by a friend) one Dr Thornton, who s[ai]th it is not a naturall distemper, that he is troubled with, but hath some hurt by an evil tongue, he s[ai]th he will not prescribe any medicine for him, until his water [i.e., urine] have been tryed by fire – i.e., they must take hi water and make a cake or loaf of it, with wheat meal, and put some of his hair into it and horse shoe stumps, and then put it in the fire, and till she or he or some doe this he will prescribe nothing for him – not that he bids her say any words yet she feared it may be some kind of charm, and as she piously expressed herself (for I hope she is a good woman), 'I being afraid to offend God by such a tryall as he prescribes, I come purposely to you and Mr Dawson to get your judgement' – Mr D. came to me the morning after to consult about it, we have concluded it not to be any way of God, having no foundation either in nature or divine revelation in scripture, I went to Halifax that day to a funeral, called of her, told her our thoughts, and then perceived their imagination, that upon their using these means, the

witch that had hurt them would come and discover all – I utterly dis-
liked it, so did her husband and she – I told them the right way was to
goe to God by fasting and prayer, they consent, we appointed yesterday,
w[hi]ch was Wednesday May 16 1683.

*The Rev Oliver Heywood B.A. 1630–1702; his Autobiography, Diaries, Anecdote and Event
Books*, ed. J. Horsfall Turner, 4 vols (Brighouse, 1882–85), vol. 4, pp. 53–4.

DOCUMENT 14   A CUNNING MAN, 1652

*There was probably no such thing as a typical cunning man, but one suspects
that this example was less typical than most. Note the gendered nature of his
business, and the way his reputation seems to have spread rapidly locally.*

West Rideing of the County of Yorke. The informacon of Lancelot Milner
of Nesfield in the said county husbandman, taken upon oath the eleventh
of March 1651[2], before Charles Fairfax of Menston, Esquire, one of the
Justices of Peace within the sayd Rydeing.

Sayth that on Weddensday was sevenight att night a man whose name he
knoweth not but p[re]tending [i.e., claiming] himselfe to be dumbe and
deafe, did come to this informer's home and stayed there a weeke in which
tyme divers from severall p[ar]tes of the country came to enquire, the
wenches what husbandes they should have; when they should come;
whether they should bee widdowes; and divers such like questions; some
men to enquire of stollen horses, or mayres, all which questions hee
answered by signes in chalke, and poyntinge with his hand which way
they were gone; and divers such p[er]sons soe directed, have tould this informer that the sayd dumbe man did directe them very truly. And of those
p[er]sons soe resortinge to him, of some of them hee tooke a penny, of
others twopence, of others a can of ale and of some nothinge; hee further
sayth that a souldier (very familiar with him) came the last weeke to this
informer's house and sayd the sayd dumbe man was borne about London.

[Information of Edward, son of Lancelot Milner, taken as above]
Sayth that within the weeke before this his informacon, a man dwelling
in or neare Rippon came to the dumbe man to enquire of a stolne mayre,
and before any discourse with the man, he the sayd dumbe p[er]son tooke

a stolle betwixt his legges and spurned it, and poynted towardes him that came to enquire of him; then tooke upp a chipp and flunge it from him, makeinge signes that it was to noe purpose to looke after her; of some he tooke a penny, of others nothing but ale; and of divers nothing at all.

[Information of Isabel Bearing of Menston, 13 March 1652]
Sayth that shee goeinge on Satterday last with others to the house of Lancelot Milner where the dumbe man was, diverse resorted thither and amongst the rest two from Tadcaster about a horse stollen and some from Morton towneshipp & others from other p[ar]tes of the county to whome he made signes by chalke upon a table and diverse gave him twopence apiece of their owne voluntary will, but shee sayth that the sayd dumbe man to her knowledge demanded nothinge of any either by signes or otherwise.

Public Record Office, London, Clerks of Assize Records,
Northern Circuit Depositions, ASSI 45/4/2/70.

Document 15   MEETING THE DEVIL AND GOING TO THE SABBAT, LANCASHIRE 1634

Part of a deposition taken by local justices from one of the women sucked into the Lancashire witch-scare of 1633–64. It contains what was to become the standard story of meeting the devil and making the pact with him, including sexual intercourse, as well as, for England, an early and rare account of the sabbat. But note how, at this point, the devil of the learned demonologist is still being conflated with the familiar spirit of popular imagination.

The Examinacon and Voluntary Confession of Margaret Johnson, widdow, taken at Padeam [Padiham] ye 9th day of March 1633 [i.e., 1634] before Richard Shuttleworth and J[oh]n Starkey, Esq, 2 of his Ma[jes]ties justicies of the peace within the county of Lancaster

Who saith that betweene 7 or 8 yeares since she beeing in her house at Marsden in great passion & anger & distracted & withall oppressed w[i]th some want there appeared unto her a spirit or devill in the similitude or proportion of a man apparrelled in a suite of blacke tied about w[i]th silke pointes [i.e., laces], whoe offered her yf shee would give him her soule, hee would supply all her wants and bring her whatsoever she wanted or needed and at her appointm[en]t would helpe her to kill & revenge her either of man or beaste or what she desired, and after a sollicitacon or two shee contracted and coadioned w[i]th the said devill or spiritt for her soule. And the said devill had her call him by the name of Mamillion, & when shee called hee would bee ready to doe her will. And she saith that in all her talke and conference shee called the said Mamillion her God. And shee further saith that the said spiritt or devill did by her consent defile her body by com[m]itting wicked uncleaness together. And she further saith that shee was not at the greate meetinge of the witches at Harestones in the Forest of Pendle on All S[ain]ts Day last past, but saith that shee was at a second meetinge the Sunday after All S[ain]ts day at the place aforesaid where there was at that time betweene 30 and 40 witches who did all ride to the said meetinge. And th'end of the said meetinge was to consult for the killing and hurting of man & beasts, and that there was one devill or spiritt that was more greate & grand devill then the rest. . . . And further saith that the devill can raise foule wether and stormes, and soe hee did at their meetinge. And shee further saith that when the devill came to suck her pappe, hee came to her in the liknes of a catt, sometimes of one collour & sometimes of another. And since this trouble befell her her spiritt hath left her and shee never sawe him since.

British Library, Additional MSS 36674, f. 196.

DOCUMENT 16   GOING TO THE SABBAT, 1673

This is an extract from the first of a series of remarkable depositions given by a woman called Ann Armstrong to the Northumberland justices in the spring of 1673. Armstrong gave several descriptions of visits to the sabbat, and named numerous people in the area as being witches who had attended these meetings. As far as is known, no trials followed these allegations. In the earlier part of this, her first, deposition, Armstrong had described meeting 'an old man with ragged cloth[e]s', clearly the devil, after which she fell into trances and fits.

Northumberl[an]d. The informacon of Ann Armstrong of Birks-nooke in the county aforesaid taken upon oath the 5th day of February 1672 [3].

And whilst she was lying in that condition which happened one night a little before Christmas about ye change of ye moone this inform[er] see the s[ai]d Anne Forster come w[i]th a bridle and bridled her and ridd upon this inform[er] crosse-legg'd till they came to [the] rest of her companions at Rideing Millne bridge where they usually mett and when she light of[f] her back pull'd the bridle of[f] this inform[er]'s head now in the likenesse of a horse, but when the bridle was taken of[f] she stood up in her owne shape, and then she see the s[ai]d Anne Forster, Anne Dryden of Pudhoe and Luce Thompson of Mickley and tenn more unkowne to this inform[er] and a long black man rideing a bay galloway as she thought which they called their protector and when they had hankt theire horses they stood all upon a bare spott off ground and bid this inform[er] sing whilst they dansed in severall shapes first of a haire then of their owne and then in a catt sometimes in a mouse and severall other shapes and when they had done, bridled this inform[er] and the rest of the horses and rid home with their protector first. And for six or seven nights together they did the same and the last night this inform[er] was with them when they mett at a house called ye Rideing house where she saw Forster, Dryden and Thompson and ye rest and their protector which they call'd their god sitting at ye head of ye table in a gold chaire as she thought and a rope hanging over the roome w[hi]ch every one touch'd three several times and whatever was desired was set upon the table of several kindes of meate and drinke and when they had eaten she that was last drew the table & kept the reversions, this was their custome w[hi]ch they usualy did.

Public Record Office, London, Clerks of Assize Records,
Northern Circuit Depositions, ASSI 45/10/3/34.

DOCUMENT 17   DEMONIC POSSESSION IN CHESHIRE, 1602

This is a classic description of the symptoms of demonic possession, in this instance as suffered by twelve-year-old Thomas Harrison of Northwich in Cheshire. The account comes from a biography of the puritan gentleman John Bruen (1560–1625), and is closely based on notes about the boy's condition made by Bruen, who was among those who prayed for Harrison's recovery. The bishop of Chester at the time was Richard Vaughan.

By his torments he was brought so low, weak, and feeble, that he was almost nothing but skin and bones, yet for the space of four and twenty hours every day (having only one half hour respite, which they called his awakening time, and wherein they gave him a little food) he was of that extraordinary strength, that if he foulded his hands together, no man could pull them asunder: if he rolled his head, or tossed his whole body (as usually he did) no man could stay, or restrain him: he would, to the great astonishment of the hearers, howl like a dog, mew like a cat, roar like a bear, froth like a boar: when any prayed with him, his passions were strongest, and his rage, and violence greatest, ready to fly in their faces, and to drown their voices by his yellings, and out-cries: if one came near him with a bible, though under his cloak, and never so secret, he would run upon him, and use great violence to get it from him, and when he could get any, he rent them in pieces: sometimes, he would lie along, as if he had been stark dead, his colour gone, and mouth so wide open, that he would on a sudden thrust both his hands into it: and notwithstanding his great weakness, he would leap and skip from his bed to the window, from the window to the table, and so to bed again, and that with such agility, as no tumbler could do the like. And yet all this while his legs were grown up so close to his buttocks, so that he could not use them: sometimes we saw his chin drawn up to his nose, that his mouth could scarce be seen: sometimes his chin and forehead drawn almost together like a bended bow; his countenance fearful by yawning, mowing, &c . . . this bishop granted a licence for a private fast in the child's father's house, for his help and release.

> Samuel Clarke, *The Second Part of the Marrow of Ecclesiastical History; containing the lives of many eminent Christians, which have lived since the primitive Times to this present Age* (London, 1675), book 2, pp. 94–5.

DOCUMENT 18   RICHARD BERNARD ON THE WITCH'S MARK, 1627

This, from one of the standard English demonological works, comes at the beginning of a discussion on what 'evidences' can prove somebody is a witch.

By a witches marke, which is upon these baser sort of witches, and by this sucking, or otherwise by the devil's touching, experience proveth the truth of this, and innumerable instances are brought for examples. Tertullian found this true, and saieth 'It is the Devil's custome to marke his: God hath his marke for his', Ezekiel 9. Rev 7 and 14. 'The Beast will have his marke', Re. 13 (who is the Devil's Lieutenant) so the Devil himself will have his mark: see the relations of witches, & the witnes of many learned men, writing of witches and witchcraft. Therefore where this marke is, here is a league and a familiar spirit.

Search diligently therefore for it in every place, and lest one be deceived by a naturall mark, note this, from that. This is insensible, and being pricked will not bleede. When the mark therefore is found, try it, but so as the witch perceive it not, seeming as not to have found it, and then let one pricke in some other places, and another in the meane space there: it's sometimes like a little teate, sometimes but a blewish spot, sometimes red spots like a fleabiting, sometimes the flesh is sunke in and hollow, as a famous witch confessed, who also said, witches cover them, and some have confessed, that they have bin taken away; but saieth that witch, they grow againe, and come to their old forme. And therefore, though this marke be not found at first, yet it may at length: once searching therefore must not serve: for some out of feare, some other for favour, make a negiligent search. It is fit therefore searchers should bee sworne to search, & search very diligently, in such a case of life and death, and for the detection of so great an height of impiety.

Richard Bernard, *A Guide to Grand Iury Men:*
divided into Two Bookes (1627), pp. 218–20.

DOCUMENT 19   SEARCHING FOR THE WITCH'S MARK, 1650

This is a typical deposition from a group of women appointed to search for the mark, taken by an Essex justice of the peace. Martha Cannon's statement shows how a suspected witch's solicitations could be as terrifying as her outright hostility.

The Informat[io]n of Anne Stanes, Mary Leaper, Mary Cooke, Margery Silvest[e]r, appointed for ye searching of Deborah Nayler upon ye suspic[io]n of witchcraft taken upon oath before me June ye 12th An[n]o Dom[ini] 1650

Anne Stanes: Informeth upon oath that she found a marke upon her body (of ye s[ai]d Deborah Nayler) in her private partes w[hi]ch she attesteth that shee nev[e]r see ye like before.

Margery [sic] Leaper: Informeth that she found 3 markes in her body somewhat more apparent then any other parte of her body & seemeing in ye p[ro]portions of a grape & another like a teate in her private partes.

Mary Cooke: Informeth upon oath that she see 2 markes in ye private partes of her body & alsoe another marke somewhat like & in ye propor[tio]n of a teate.

Margery Silvest[e]r: Informeth ye same upon oath.

The Information of Martha Common of Debenham taken upon oath before me June ye 12th An[n]o Dom[ini] 1650.

That ye s[ai]d Deborah Nayler came to her howse & prayed for theyr healthes saying that she see an ill signe about ye house that betokened a sickness or death of some of the howse. Upon demaund s[ai]d that it was a herne [heron] & that imediately she ye s[ai]d Mrs Cannon fell dangerously sicke & came not out of her chamb[e]r for ye space of halfe a yeare togeather.

Christo[pher] Muschamp.

Essex Record Office, Quarter Sessions Bundles, Q/SBa 2/74.

Document 20 WITCHCRAFT, FEMALE SOCIAL SPACE, AND WOMEN

A document which shows witchcraft suspicions running between women, with the welfare of a child as the central issue. Despite the title of the pamphlet this extract comes from, the case was tried in 1662, and is noteworthy because of the involvement of Sir Matthew Hale, the leading judge of the day, and of the eminent doctor Sir Thomas Browne, who gave medical evidence for the prosecution. Amy Duny [Denny], probably in her early fifties when the trial took place, was found guilty and executed, as was the other woman accused, Rose Cullender.

As concerning William Durent, being an infant, his mother Dorothy Durent sworn and examined, deposed in open court, that about the tenth of March, *nono Caroli Secundi* [i.e., 1658], she having a special occasion to go from home, and having none in her house to take care of her child (it then sucking) desired Amy Duny her neighbour, to look to her child during her absence, for which she promised her to give her a penny: but the said Dorothy Durent desired the said Amy not to suckle her child, and laid a great charge upon her not to do it. Upon which it was asked by the court, why she did give that direction, being an old woman and not capable of giving suck? It was answered by the said Dorothy Durent, that she very well knew that she did not give suck, but that for some years before, she had gone under the reputation of a witch, which was one cause made her give her the caution: another was, that it was customary with old women, that if they did look after a sucking child, and nothing would please it but the breast, they did use to please the child, to give it the breast, and it did please the child, but it sucked nothing but wind, which did the child hurt. Nevertheless after the departure of this deponent, the said Amy did suckle the child: and after the return of the said Dorothy, the said Amy did acquaint her, that she had given suck to the child, contrary to her command. Whereupon the deponent was very angry with the said Amy for the same; at which the said Amy was much discontented, and used many high expressions and threatening speeches towards her, telling her that she had as good to have done otherwise than to have found fault with her, and so departed out of her house. And that very night her son fell into strange fits of swounding, and was held in such terrible manner, that she was much affrighted therewith, and so continued for divers weeks.

A Tryal of Witches, at the Assizes held at Bury St. Edmunds for the County of Suffolk; on the Tenth day of March, 1664. Before Sir Matthew Hale, Kt., then Lord Chief Baron of His Majesties Court of Exchequer (1682), pp. 2–5.

DOCUMENT 21   ESSEX, 1645: A WITCH FINDER GIVES EVIDENCE

This is part of a printed version of evidence given to local justices by Matthew Hopkins, at the beginning of the 1645–47 witch-hunts. Note the references to 'watching', which involved keeping suspects awake in hopes that their familiars would come to them, to sexual intercourse with the devil, and to Hopkins' associate John Stearne. The deposition continues with more on familiars. Elizabeth Clarke, along with perhaps eighteen other women, was hanged at Chelmsford in July 1645.

The information of Matthew Hopkins of Mannintree [Manningtree], Gent., taken upon oath the 25th day of March 1645.

The informant saieth, that the said Elizabeth Clarke (suspected for a witch as aforesaid) being by the appointment of the said justices watched certaine nights, for the better discovery of her wicked practices, this informant came into the roome where the said Elizabeth was watched, as aforesaid, the last night, being the 24th of this instant March, but intended not to have stayed long there. But the said Elizabeth forth with told this informant and one master Sterne there present, if they would stay and do the said Elizabeth no hurt, shee would call one of her white impes, and play with it in her lap; but this informant told her, they would not allow of it; and that staying there a while longer, the said Elizabeth confessed shee had had carnall copulation with the devill six or seven yeares; and that he would appeare to her three of foure times in a weeke at her bed side, and goe to bed with her, and lye with her halfe a night together in the shape of a proper gentleman, with a laced band, having the whole proportion of a man, and would say to her 'Besse I must lye with you', and shee did never deny him. And within a quarter of an houre after there appeared an impe like to a dog, which was white, with some sandy spots, and seemed to be very fat and plumpe, with very short legges, who forthwith vanished away: and the said Elizabeth said the name of the impe was, Jarmara: and immediately there appeared another impe, which shee called Vinegar Tom, in the shape of a greyhound with long legges: and the said Elizabeth then said that the next impe should be a black impe, and should come for the said master Sterne, which appeared, but presently vanished: and the last that appeared was in the shape of a polcat, but the head somewhat bigger.

A true and exact Relation of the severall Informations, Examinations and Confessions of the late Witches arraigned and executed in the late Sessions holden before the Right Honorable Robert, Earl of Warwicke, and severall of his Majesties Justices of Peace, the 29 of July 1645 (1645), p. 2.

DOCUMENT 22 MATTHEW HOPKINS DEFENDS HIS ACTIONS

In 1647 Hopkins published a tract written 'in answer to several queries' about his investigative techniques which had been raised with the assize judges in Norfolk: here are his answers to charges, firstly, that he was a 'torturing witch-catcher who forced confessions by threats or deception' (query 11), and, secondly, that his major objective was to 'fleece the country of their money' by making a profit from witch-hunting (query 14).

Answer [to query 11]. He is of a better conscience, and for your better understanding of him, he doth thus uncase himselfe to all, and declares what confessions (though made by a witch against her selfe) he allows not of, and doth altogether account of no validity, or worthy of credence to be given to it, and ever did so account it, and ever likewise shall.

1. He utterly denyes that confession of a witch to be of any validity, when it is drawn from her by any torture or violence whatsoever: although after watching, walking or swimming, diverse have suffered, yet peradventure magistrates with much care and diligence did solely and fully examine them after sleepe, and consideration sufficient.
2. He utterly denyes that confession of a witch, which is drawn from her by flattery, viz 'If you will confesse you shall go home, you shall not go to the gaole, nor be hanged, &c'.
3. He utterly denyes that confession of a witch, when she confesseth any improbabilty, impossibility, as flying in the ayre, riding on a broom, &c.
4. He utterly denyes a confession of a witch, when it is interrogated to her, and words put into her mouth, to be of any force or effect: as to

say to a silly [i.e., simple-minded] (yet witch wicked enough), 'You
have foure imps have you not?' She answers affirmatively, 'Yes': 'Did
they not suck you?' 'Yes', saieth she: 'Are not their names so, and
so?' 'Yes', saith shee: 'Did you not send such an impe to kill my
child?' 'Yes', saith she, this being all her confession, after this manner, it is by him accompted nothing, and he earnestly doth desire
that all magistrates and jurors would a little more then ever they did,
examine witnesses, about the interrogated confessions.

Answer [to query 14]. You doe him a great deale of wrong in every of
these particulars. For, first,

1. He never went to any towne or place, but they rode, writ, or sent
   often for him, and were (for ought he knew) glad of him.
2. He is a man that doth disclaime that ever he detected a witch, or
   said, 'Thou art a witch'; only after her tryall by search, and their
   owne confessions, he as others may judge.
3. Lastly, judge how he fleeceth the country, and inriches himself, by
   considering the vast summe he takes of every towne, he demands
   20.s. a town, and doth sometimes ride 20 miles for that, & hath no
   more for all his charges thither and back again (& it may be stayes a
   weeke there) and finde there 3. or 4. Witches, or if it be but one,
   cheap enough, and this is the great summe he takes to maintaine his
   companie with 3. horses.

> Matthew Hopkins, *The Discovery of Witches: in Answer to severall Queries,*
> *lately delivered to the Judges of Assize for the County of Norfolk,*
> *1647* (1647), pp. 7–8, 9–10.

DOCUMENT 23 CONVICTIONS FOR WITCHCRAFT AND POLITICAL EXPEDIENCY, 1682

This is part of a letter dated 19 August 1682 from Lord Chief Justice Sir
Francis North (1637–85) to Secretary of State Sir Leoline Jenkins describing the
trial of three women condemned and executed as witches at Exeter. The re-
mainder of the letter is concerned with the effective running of government in
the south-west.

Here have been three old women condemned for witchcraft. Your curiosity will make you enquire of their circumstances. I shall only tell you what I had from my brother Raymond [i.e., Sir Thomas Raymond, the judge presiding over the trial], before whom they were tried, that they were the most old, decrepid, despicable, miserable creatures that ever he saw. A painter would have chosen them out of the whole country for figures of that kind to have drawn by. The evidence against them was very full and fanciful, but their own confessions exceeded it. They appeared not only weary of their lives but to have a great deal of skill to convict themselves. Their description of sucking devils with saucer eyes were so natural that the jury could not choose but believe them. I find the country so fully possessed against them that, though some of the virtuosi may think these things the effects of confederacy, melancholy or delusion and that young folks are altogether as quicksighted as they who are old and infirm, yet we cannot reprieve them without appearing to deny the very being of witches, as it is contrary to the law, so I think it would be ill for his Majesty's service, for it may give the faction [i.e., the Whig/nonconformist interest] occasion to set afoot the old trade of witch finding, that may cost many innocent persons their lives, which this justice will prevent.

Calendar of State Papers, Domestic Series, January 1st to December 31st, 1682, ed.
F.H. Blackburne Daniell (London, 1932), p. 347.

DOCUMENT 24 JOSEPH GLANVILL DEFENDS WITCH BELIEFS

Joseph Glanvill's Saducismus Triumphatus *was an important defence of the belief in witchcraft which was to remain influential well into the eighteenth century. In the two passages below we find Glanvill firstly stating what was to become the standard argument against those denying the existence of witches, that maintaining witch beliefs was vital to the maintenance of Christianity and, secondly, demonstrating how heavily the weight of both tradition and observation supported the belief in witchcraft.*

That though philosophical discourses to justifie the common belief about witches, are nothing at all to them [i.e., sceptics], or those of their measure; yet they are too seasonable and necessary for our age, in which atheism is begun in Sadducism: and those that dare not bluntly say, there is no God, content themselves (for a fair step and introduction) to deny there are spirits, or witches. Which sort of infidels, though they are not ordinary among the meer vulgar, yet are they numerous in a little higher rank of understandings. And those that know any thing of the world, know, that most of the looser gentry, and the small pretenders to philosophy and wit, are generally deriders of the belief of witches and apparitions. And were this a light and slight or mere speculative mistake, I should not trouble my self or them about it. But I fear this errour hath a core in it that is worse than heresie: and therefore how little soever I care what men believe or teach in matters of opinion, I think I have reason to be concern'd in an affair that toucheth so near the general interests of religion. . . .

And in order to the proof that there have been, and are, unlawful confederacies with evil spirits, by virtue of which the hellish accomplices [i.e., witches] perform things above their natural powers: I must premise, that this being matter of fact, is onely capable of the evidence of authority and sense; and by both these the being of witches and diabolical contracts is most abundantly confirm'd. All histories are full of the exploits of those instruments of darkness; and the testimony of ages, not onely of the rude and barbarous, but of the most civiliz'd and polish'd world, brings tidings of their strange performances. We have the attestations of thousands of eye and ear-witnesses, and those not of the easily-deceivable vulgar onely, but of wise and grave discerners; and that, when no interest could oblige them to agree together in a common lye. I say, we have the light of all these circumstances to confirm us in the belief of things done by persons of despicable power and knowledge, beyond the reach of art and ordinary nature.

Joseph Glanvill, *Saducismus Triumphatus: or full and plain Evidence concerning Witches and Apparitions* (1681), pt 1, 'Preface', sigs F2v–F3; pp. 4–5.

DOCUMENT 25   WITCH-HUNTING ADVOCATED, 1722

Richard Boulton's work of 1722 was the last major statement in support of witch beliefs by an English author. It consisted of a point-by-point refutation of

Francis Hutchinson's attack on Boulton's Compleat History of Magick, Sorcery and Witchcraft *of 1715, rounded off with a lengthy discussion of the influence of immaterial substances on the material world. Having proved the existence of witches to his own satisfaction, Boulton ended his book by calling for action against them.*

I shall therefore conclude this chapter, with this observation further, of the nature and power of these diabolical spirits, who are the chief actors of these tragical arts of witchcraft, &c, viz. That as they can insinuate their ill representations into the minds of men, and torture their bodies, so they have power to assume bodies when they please, and appear in different shapes: as when the devil enter'd the swine, and transformed himself into an angel of light. And angels not only appeared upon several occasions, but our saviour told his disciples to feel that he had flesh and bones; which he needed not to have distinguished himself by, if spirits could not render themselves visible; he would have said that spirits could not appear.

Since then it appears, that the art of witchcraft is not impossible, but hath the testimony of reason, as well as other proof: all I shall add is, that as God spared not angels that sinned, nor Adam that transgressed, and hath strictly commanded that a witch should not live, the laws against such persons ought to be put in execution, lest we disobey God, and in excusing horrible crimes, suffer the world to be overrun with wickedness.

> Richard Boulton, *The Possibility and Reality of Magick, Sorcery and Witchcraft*
> *demonstrated. Or, a Vindication of a Compleat History of Magick,*
> *Sorcery and Witchcraft* (1722), p. 184.

DOCUMENT 26   REFUTING WITCH BELIEFS, 1736

This is an extract from a sermon preached in 1736, coincidentally very shortly after the repeal of the witchcraft Acts, by a country vicar alarmed that a witch had been swum by his parishioners. His arguments against the belief in witchcraft were mainly familiar ones, and the sentiments expressed here should be compared with those expressed 150 years earlier by Reginald Scot [Doc. 4].

Juxon is criticizing 'the truth and wisdom of modern notions of witchcraft, which have no foundation than ignorance or superstition'.

It is then not only a great weakness, but great sinfulness to ascribe so much as many are inclined to do to diabolical powers: it is giving the God of truth the lye; it is a flat denial of his government of the world, and of the wisdom and goodness of his providence; it is exalting infernal spirits into the seat of God, and assigning 'em a commission to scatter plagues and curses throughout the world, from that throne where to our comfort the sovereign lord of the universe sits, and reigns to shower down his blessings upon us. But surely where any are so weak, or so wicked as this, after they have thus provoked the God of heaven to forsake 'em, there can be no occasion to have recourse to witchcraft, in order to account for any evils that are suffered to befall 'em, and much less so, where these evils are such as may proceed from natural causes, and are common unto men. Is it not most intolerable that mere natural effects, or the divine judgements upon us for our sins, instead of teaching us to reform our lives, should only teach us more and more to dishonour the name of God, to magnify the power of his greatest enemy, and to take away the good name, or perhaps seek the life of those, who have neither inclination nor power to do us any evil.

Joseph Juxon, *A Sermon upon Witchcraft. Occasion'd by a late illegal Attempt to discover Witches by Swimming, preach'd at Twyford, in the County of Leicester, July 11, 1736* (1736), pp. 22–3.

DOCUMENT 27   SOME EIGHTEENTH-CENTURY COMMENTS

These three extracts demonstrate how educated opinion in the eighteenth century had great difficulty in totally rejecting witchcraft beliefs. The passage from the essayist Joseph Addison (1672–1719) probably echoes what many observers felt in the early eighteenth century. It is, however, odd to see a similar ambivalence being expressed, and Addison's opinions alluded to, by the great English jurist Sir William Blackstone (1723–80: the first edition of his Commentaries *appeared between 1765 and 1769). Finally, the comments of John Wesley (1707–91), the founder of Methodism, show how even in the late eighteenth century the position defended by Glanvill a century earlier was still regarded as valid by at least one remarkable Christian thinker. Wesley wrote this passage after interviewing Elizabeth Hobson, a young woman from Sunderland, about her supernatural experiences.*

There are some opinions in which a man should stand neuter, without engaging his assent to one side or the other. Such a hovering faith as this, which refuses to settle upon any determination, is absolutely necessary in a mind that is careful to avoid errors and prepossessions. When the arguments press equally on both sides in matters that are indifferent to us, the safest method is to give up our selves to neither.

It is with this temper of mind that I consider the subject of witchcraft. When I hear the relations that are made from all parts of the world, not only from Norway and Lapland, from the East and West Indies, but from every particular nation in Europe, I cannot forbear thinking that there is such an intercourse and commerce with evil spirits, as that which we express by the name of witchcraft. But when I consider that the ignorant and credulous parts of the world abound most in these relations, and that the persons among us who are supposed to engage in such an infernal commerce are people of a weak understanding and crazed imagination, and at the same time reflect upon the many impostures and delusions of this nature that have been detected in all ages, I endeavour to suspend my belief till I hear more certain accounts than any which have yet come to my knowledge. In short, when I consider the question, whether there are such persons in the world as those we call witches? My mind is divided between the two opposite opinions; or rather (to speak my thoughts freely) I believe in general, that there is, and has been such a thing as witchcraft; but at the same time can give no credit to any particular instance of it.

Joseph Addison, *The Spectator*, 14 July 1711.

A sixth species of offences against God and religion, of which our ancient books are full, is a crime of which one knows not well what account to give. I mean the offence of witchcraft, conjuration, enchantment or sorcery. To deny the possibility, nay, actual existence, of witchcraft and sorcery, is at once flatly to contradict the revealed word of God, in various passages both of the old and the new testament: and the thing itself is a truth to which every nation in the world hath in its turn borne testimony, either by examples seemingly well attested, or by prohibitory laws, which at least suppose the possibility of a commerce with evil spirits ... indeed the ridiculous stories that are generally told, and many impostures and delusions that have been discovered in all ages, are enough to demolish all faith in such a dubious crime; if the contrary evidence were not also extremely strong. Wherefore it seems to be the most eligible way to conclude, with an ingenious writer of our own, that in general there has been such a thing as witchcraft; though one cannot give credit to any particular modern instance of it.

William Blackstone, *Commentaries on the Laws of England*,

4 vols, 5th edn, Oxford, 1773, vol. 4, pp. 60–1.

It is true, likewise, that the English in general, and indeed most of the men of learning in Europe, have given up all accounts of witches and apparitions, as mere old wives fables. I am sorry for it; and I willingly take the opportunity of entering my solemn protest against this violent compliment which so many that believe in the Bible pay to those who do not believe it. I owe them no such service. I take knowledge these are at the bottom of the outcry which has been raised, and with such insolence spread throughout the nation, in direct opposition not only to the Bible, but to the suffrage of the wisest and best of men in all ages and nations. They well know (whether Christians know it or not), that the giving up witchcraft is, in effect, giving up the Bible; and they know, on the other hand, that if but one account of the intercourse of men with separate spirits be admitted, their whole castle in the air (Deism, Atheism, Materialism) falls to the ground. I know no reason, therefore, why we should suffer even this weapon to be wrested out of our hands. Indeed there are numerous arguments besides, which abundantly confute their vain imaginations. But we need not be hooted out of one; neither reason nor religion require this.

The Journal of the Rev. John Wesley, A.M., ed. Nehemiah

Curnock, 8 vols (1909–16), vol. 5, p. 265.

Bibliography

The place of publication is London unless otherwise stated.

Early modern English works on witchcraft and demonology

1   Ady, T., *A Candle in the Dark: or, a Treatise concerning the Nature of Witches and Witchcraft: being Advice to Judges, Sheriffes, Justices of the Peace, and Grand Jury Men, what to do, before they passe sentence on such as are arraigned for their Lives, as Witches*, 1656.*

2   *The Apprehension and Confession of three notorious Witches. Arraigned and by Justice condemnede and executed at Chelmesforde in the Countye of Essex, the 5 Day of July last past 1589*, 1589.

3   Bernard, R., *A Guide to Grand Iury Men: divided into two Bookes*, 1627.

4   Boulton, R., *A Compleat History of Magick, Sorcery and Witchcraft*, 2 vols, 1715.

5   Boulton, R., *The Possibility and Reality of Magick, Sorcery and Witchcraft demonstrated. Or, a Vindication of a Compleat History of Magick, Sorcery and Witchcraft*, 1722.

6   Bovet, R., *Pandaemonium, or the Devil's Cloyster. Being a further Blow to modern Sadduceism, proving the Existence of Witches and Spirits*, 1684.

7   *The Boy of Bilson: or a true Discovery of the late notorious Imposture of certaine Romish Priests in their pretended Exorcisme, or Expulsion of the Divell out of a young Boy, named William Perry*, 1622.

8   Casaubon, M., *Of Credulity and Incredulity in Things natural, civil and divine*, 1668.

9   *The Case of Hertfordshire Witchcraft consider'd: being an Examination of a Book, entitl'd, a full and impartial Account of the Discovery of Sorcery & Witchcraft practis'd by Jane Wenham of Walkerne in Hertfordshire, upon the Bodies of Anne Thorne, Anne Street, &c.*, 1712.

10   Cooper, T., *The Mystery of Witch-Craft: discovering the Truth, Nature, Occasions, Growth and Power thereof: together with the Detection and Punishment of the same*, 1617.

11   Cotta, J., *The infallible, true, and assured Witch: or, the second Edition of the Tryall of Witchcraft: shewing the right and true Method of the Discoverie*, 1625.

12   *Daemonologia: a Discourse on Witchcraft, as it was acted in the Family of Mr. Edward Fairfax, of Fuyston, in the County of York, in the Year 1621: along with the only two Eclogues of the same author known to be in Existence*, ed. William Grainge, Harrogate, 1882.

13   Darrell, J., *A true Narration of the strange and grevous Vexation by the Devil, of 7 Persons in Lancashire, and William Somers of Nottingham*, 1600.

14   Davenport, J., *The Witches of Huntingdon, their Examinations and Confessions, exactly taken by his Majesties Justices of the Peace for that County*, 1645.

15   Denison, J., *The most wonderfull and true storie of a certaine Witch named Alse Gooderidge of Stapenhill, who was arraigned and convicted at Darbie at the Assises there*, 1597.

16   *A Detection of damnable Driftes, practized by three Witches arraigned at Chelmisforde in Essex, at the late Assizes holden, which were executed in Aprill 1579*, 1579.

17   *The Examination and Confession of certaine Wytches at Chensforde in the Countie of Essex, before the Quenes Maiesties Judges, the xxvi day of July Anno 1566*, 1566.

18   *The Examination of John Walsh, before Maister Thomas Williams, Commissary to the Reverend Father of God William, Bishop of Excester, upon certayne Interrogatories touchyng Wytchcrafte and Sorcerye*, 1566.

19   Filmer, R., *An Advertisement to the Jurymen of England, touching Witches. Together with a Difference between an English and an Hebrew Witch*, 1653.

20   *A full and impartial Account of the Discovery of Sorcery and Witchcraft practis'd by Jane Wenham of Walkerne in Hertfordshire, upon the Bodies of Anne Thorne, Anne Street, &c.*, 1712.

21   Gaule, J., *Select Cases of Conscience touching Witches and Witchcrafts*, 1646.

22   Gifford, G., *A Dialogue concerning Witches and Withcrafts, in which it is layed open how craftily the Divell deceiveth not onely the Witches but many Other, and so leadeth them awrie into manie great Errours*, 1593.

23   Glanvill, J., *Saducismus Triumphatus: or full and plain Evidence concerning Witches and Apparitions*, 1681.

24   Goodcole, H., *The wonderfull Discoverie of Elizabeth Sawyer a Witch, late of Edmonton, her Conviction and Condemnation and Death*, 1621.

25   Harsnett, S., *A Declaration of egregious popish Impostures, to with-draw the Harts of her Maiesties Subiects from their Allegeance and from the Truth of the Christian Religion as professed in England, under the Pretence of Casting out Devils*, 1603.

26   Harsnett, S., *A Discovery of the fraudulent Practices of John Darrell Bachelor of Artes*, 1599.

27   Holland, H., *A Treatise against Witchcraft: or, a Dialogue, wherein the greatest Doubts concerning that Sinne, are briefly answered*, Cambridge, 1590.

28   Hopkins, M., *The Discovery of Witches: in Answer to severall Queries, lately delivered to the Judges of Assize for the County of Norfolk, 1647*, 1647.

29   Hutchinson, F., *An historical Essay concerning Witchcraft. With Observations of Matters of Fact, tending to clear the Texts of the sacred Scriptures, and confute the vulgar Errors about that Point*, 1718.

30 Juxon, J., *A Sermon upon Witchcraft: Occasion'd by a late illegal Attempt to discover Witches by Swimming. Preach'd at Twyford in the County of Leicester, July 11, 1736*, 1736.

31 *The Life and Conversation of Temperance Floyd, Mary Lloyd, and Susanna Edwards, three eminent Witches lately condemned at Exeter Assizes*, 1682.

32 Moore, M., *Wonderfull News from the North: or, a true Relation of the sad and grievous Torments, inflicted upon the Bodies of three Children of Mr George Muschamp, late of the County of Northumberland, by Witchcraft*, 1650.

33 More, H., *An Antidote against Atheisme: or an Appeal to the natural Faculties of the Minde of Men, whether there be not a God*, 1653.

34 *The most strange and admirable Discoverie of the three Witches at Warboys arraigned, convicted and executed at the last Assizes at Huntingdon*, 1593.

35 *Newes from Scotland: declaring the damnable Life and Death of Doctor Fian, a notable Sorcerer*, 1591.

36 Perkins, W., *A Discourse of the Damned Art of Witchcraft. So farre forth as it is revealed in the Scriptures, and manifest by true Experience*, Cambridge, 1608.

37 Potts, T., *The wonderfull Discoverie of Witches in the Countie of Lancaster. With the arraignment and Triall of nineteene notorious Witches, at the Assizes and generall Gaole Deliverie, holden at the Castle of Lancaster, upon Munday, the seventeenth of August last, 1612*, 1613.

38 *A Rehearsall both straung and true, of hainous and horrible Actes committed by Elizabeth Stile, alias Rockingham, Mother Dutten, Mother Devell, Mother Margaret, fower notorious Witches, apprehended at Winsore in the Countie of Barks, and at Abington arraigned, condemned, and executed the 28 Day of Februarie last Anno 1579*, 1579.

39 Roberts, A., *A Treatise of Witchcraft: wherein sundry Propositions are laid downe, plainely discovering the Wickednesse of that damnable Art*, 1616.

40 Scot, R. *The Discoverie of Witchcraft*, 1584

41 Stearne, J., *A Confirmation and Discovery of Witchcraft*, 1648.

42 *A true and exact Relation of the severall Informations, Examinations and Confessions of the late Witches arraigned and executed at the late Sessions holden before the Right Honorable Robert, Earle of Warwicke, and severall of his Majesties Justices of the Peace, the 29 of July 1645*, 1645.

43 *A true and impartial Relation of the Informations against three witches, viz Temperance Floyd, Mary Trembles, and Susanna Edwards*, 1682.

44 *A true and just Recorde, of the Information, Examination, and Confession of all the Witches taken at S. Oses in the Countie of Essex, whereof some were executed, and some entreated according to the Determination of the Lawe*, 1582.

45 *The Tryal, Condemnation, and Execution of three Witches, viz Temperance Floyd, Mary Floyd and Susanna Edwards, who were all arraigned at Exeter on the 18th of August 1682*, 1682.

46 *The Tryal of Richard Hathaway upon an Information for being a Cheat and Imposter, for endeavouring to take away the Life of Sarah Morduck, for being a Witch*, 1702.

47 *A Tryal of Witches, at the Assizes held at Bury St. Edmunds for the County of Suffolk; on the Tenth day of March 1664. Before Sir Matthew Hale, Kt., then Lord Chief Baron of his Majesties Court of Exchequer,* 1682.

48 Wagstaffe, J., *The Question of Witchcraft debated,* 1669.

49 Webster, J., *The Displaying of Supposed Witchcraft,* 1677.

50 *Witches apprehended, examined and executed, for notable Villanies by them committed both by Land and Water. With a strange and most true Triall to know whether a Woman be a Witch or not,* 1613.

Secondary works

A. Books

General Works on the History of Witchcraft

51 Ankarloo, B., and Henningsen, G. (eds), *Early Modern European Witchcraft: Centres and Peripheries,* Oxford University Press, Oxford, 1990.

52 Barry, J., Hester, M., and Roberts, G. (eds), *Witchcraft in Early Modern Europe: Studies in Culture and Belief,* Cambridge University Press, Cambridge, 1996.

53 Behringer, W., *Witchcraft Persecutions in Bavaria: Popular Magic, Religious Zealotry and Reason of State in Early Modern Europe,* Cambridge University Press, Cambridge, 1997.

54 Briggs, R., *Communities of Belief: Cultural and Social Tensions in Early Modern France,* Clarendon Press, Oxford, 1989.

55 Briggs, R., *Witches and Neighbours: the Social and Cultural Context of European Witchcraft,* Harper Collins, 1996.

56 Clark, S., *Thinking with Demons: the Idea of Witchcraft in Early Modern Europe,* Oxford University Press, Oxford, 1997.

57 Devlin, J., *The Superstitious Mind: French Peasants and the Supernatural in the Nineteenth Century,* Yale University Press, New Haven, CT, and London, 1987.

58 Eirenreich, B., and English, D., *Witches, Midwives and Nurses: a History of Women Healers,* Writers and Readers Publishing Cooperative, 1973.

59 Evans-Pritchard, E.E., *Witchcraft, Oracles and Magic among the Azande,* Clarendon Press, Oxford, 1937.

60 Favret-Saada, J., *Deadly Words: Witchcraft in the Bocage,* Cambridge University Press, Cambridge and Paris, 1980.

61 Gardiner, G.B., *Witchcraft Today,* Rider, 1954.

62 Hutton, R., *The Triumph of the Moon: a History of Modern Pagan Witchcraft,* Oxford University Press, Oxford, 1999.

63 Klaits, J., *Servants of Satan: the Age of the Witch Hunts,* Indiana University Press, Bloomington, IN, 1985.

64 Larner, C., *Enemies of God: the Witch-hunt in Scotland,* 1981.

65 Levack, B.P., *The Witch-hunt in Early Modern Europe,* 2nd edn, Longman, 1995.

66   Luhrmann, T., *Persuasions of the Witch's Craft: Ritual Magic and Witchcraft in Present-day England*, Blackwell, Oxford, 1989.

67   Michelet, Jules, *La Sorcière*, Paris, 1862.

68   Midelfort, H.C.E., *Witch Hunting in Southwestern Germany, 1562–1684: the Social and Intellectual Foundations*, Stanford University Press, Stanford, CA, 1972.

69   Murray, M., *The Witch Cult in Western Europe*, Clarendon Press, Oxford, 1921.

70   Parrinder, G., *Witchcraft: European and African*, Faber and Faber, 1963.

71   Roper, L., *Oedipus and the Devil: Witchcraft, Sexuality and Religion in Early Modern Europe*, Routledge, 1994.

72   Sanders, A., *A Deed without a Name: the Witch in Society and History*, Berg, Oxford and Washington, DC, 1995.

73   Shumaker, W. (ed.), *The Occult Sciences in the Renaissance*, University of California Press, Berkeley, Los Angeles and London, 1972.

74   Soman, A., *Sorcellerie et Justice Criminelle (16e–18e Siècles)*, Variorum, Ashgate and Brookfield, VT, 1992.

75   Trevor-Roper, H.R., *The European Witch-craze of the Sixteenth and Seventeenth Centuries*, Harmondsworth, 1969.

Works on the History of Witchcraft in England

76   Bostridge, I., *Witchcraft and its Transformations c. 1650–c. 1750*, Clarendon Press, Oxford, 1997.

77   Clulee, N.H., *John Dee's Natural Philosophy: between Science and Religion*, Routledge, 1988.

78   Corbin, P., and Sedge, D. (eds), *Three Jacobean Witchcraft Plays: Sophonisba; The Witch; The Witch of Edmonton*, Manchester University Press, Manchester, 1986.

79   Davies, O., *Witchcraft, Magic and Culture 1736–1951*, Manchester University Press, Manchester and New York, 1999.

80   Deacon, R., *Matthew Hopkins: Witch-finder General*, Frederick Muller, 1976.

81   Ewen, C.L., *Witch Hunting and Witch Trials: the Indictments for Witchcraft from the Records of 1373 Assizes held for the Home Circuit A.D. 1559–1736*, Kegan Paul, Trench, Trubner & Co., 1929.

82   Ewen, C.L., *Witchcraft and Demonianism: a Concise Account derived from Sworn Depositions and Confessions obtained in the Courts of England and Wales*, Heath Cranton Limited, 1933.

83   French, P.J., *John Dee: the World of an Elizabethan Magus*, Routledge and Kegan Paul, 1972.

84   Gaskill, M., *Crime and Mentalities in Early Modern England*, Cambridge University Press, Cambridge, 2000: pt 2, 'Witchcraft'.

85   Geiss, G., and Bunn, I., *A Trial of Witches: a Seventeenth-century Witchcraft Prosecution*, Routledge, 1997.

86   Gibson, J., *Hanged for Witchcraft: Elizabeth Lowys and her Successors*, Tudor Press, Canberra, 1988.

87   Gibson, M., *Reading Witchcraft: Stories of Early English Witches*, Routledge, 1996.
88   Harris, A., *Night's Black Agents: Witchcraft and Magic in Seventeenth-century English Drama*, Manchester University Press, Manchester, 1980.
89   Hester, M., *Lewd Women and Wicked Witches: a Study in the Dynamics of Male Domination*, Routledge, 1992.
90   Kittredge, G.L., *Witchcraft in Old and New England*, Cambridge, MA, 1929: reprinted Russell and Russell, New York, 1956.
91   Lumby, J., *The Lancashire Witch-craze: Jennet Preston and the Lancashire Witches, 1612*, Carnegie Publishing, Preston, 1995.
92   MacDonald, M., *Mystical Bedlam: Madness, Anxiety and Healing in Seventeenth-century England*, Cambridge University Press, Cambridge, 1981.
93   MacDonald, M., *Witchcraft and Hysteria in Elizabethan London: Edward Jorden and the Mary Glover Case*, Tavistock/Routledge, 1990.
94   Macfarlane, A., *Witchcraft in Tudor and Stuart England: a Regional and Comparative Study*, Routledge and Kegan Paul, 1971; reprinted Routledge, 1999.
95   Notestein, W., *A History of Witchcraft in England, from 1558 to 1718*, Washington, DC, 1911; reprinted Thomas Y. Crowell, New York, 1968.
96   Parker, D., *Familiar to All: William Lilly and Astrology in the Seventeenth Century*, Jonathan Cape, 1975.
97   Purkiss, D., *The Witch in History: Early Modern and Twentieth-century Representations*, Routledge, 1996.
98   Rickert, C.H., *The Case of John Darrell: Minister and Exorcist* (University of Florida Monographs, Humanities, 9), Gainsville, FL, 1962.
99   Rosen, B., *Witchcraft*, Edward Arnold, 1969.
100 Sharpe, J., *Instruments of Darkness: Witchcraft in England 1550–1750*, Hamish Hamilton, 1996.
101 Sharpe, J., *The Bewitching of Anne Gunter: a True and Horrible Story of Football, Murder, Witchcraft and the King of England*, Profile Books, 1999.
102 Thomas, K., *Religion and the Decline of Magic: Studies in Popular Beliefs in Sixteenth and Seventeenth-century England*, Weidenfeld and Nicolson, 1971.
103 Thompson, J.A., *Wives, Widows, Witches and Bitches: Women in Seventeenth-century Devon*, Peter Lang, New York, etc., 1993.
104 Trevor-Davies, R., *Four Centuries of Witch Beliefs: with Special Reference to the Great Rebellion*, Methuen, 1947.
105 Walker, D.P., *Unclean Spirits: Possession and Exorcism in France and England in the Late Sixteenth and Early Seventeenth Centuries*, Scolar Press, Philadelphia, PA, 1981.
106 Willis, D., *Malevolent Nurture: Witch-hunting and Maternal Power in Early Modern England*, Cornell University Press, Ithaca, NY, and London, 1995.

B.   Articles, Essays, Pamphlets, etc.

107 Anglo, S., 'Reginald Scot and his *Discoverie of Witchcraft*: scepticism and saduceeism', in S. Anglo (ed.), *The Damned Art: Essays in the Literature of Witchcraft*, Routledge and Kegan Paul, 1977.

108   Barry, J., 'Introduction: Keith Thomas and the problem of witchcraft', in J. Barry, M. Hester and G. Roberts (eds), *Witchcraft in Early Modern Europe: Studies in Culture and Belief*, Cambridge University Press, Cambridge, 1996.

109   Carnochen, W.B., 'Witch-hunting and belief in 1751: the case of Thomas Colley and Ruth Osborne', *Journal of Social History*, 4, 1970–71.

110   De Windt, A.R., 'Witchcraft and conflicting visions of the ideal village community', *Journal of British Studies*, 34, 1995.

111   Elmer, P., ' "Saints or sorcerers": quakerism, demonology and the decline of witchcraft in seventeenth-century England', in J. Barry, M. Hester and G. Roberts (eds), *Witchcraft in Early Modern Europe: Studies in Culture and Belief*, Cambridge University Press, Cambridge, 1996.

112   Estes, L.L., 'Reginald Scot and his *Discoverie of Witchcraft*: religion and science in opposition to the European witch-craze', *Church History*, 52, 1983.

113   Gaskill, M., 'Witchcraft and power in early modern England: the case of Margaret Moore', in J. Kermode and G. Walker (eds), *Women, Crime and the Courts in Early Modern England*, University College London Press, 1994.

114   Gaskill, M., 'Witchcraft in early modern Kent: stereotypes and the background to accusations', in J. Barry, M. Hester and G. Roberts (eds), *Witchcraft in Early Modern Europe: Studies in Culture and Belief*, Cambridge University Press, Cambridge, 1996.

115   Gaskill, M., 'The devil in the shape of a man: witchcraft, conflict and belief in Jacobean England', *Historical Research*, 71, 1998.

116   Gregory, A., 'Witchcraft, politics and "good neighbourhood" in early seventeenth-century Rye', *Past and Present*, 133, 1991.

117   Guskin, P.J., 'The context of English witchcraft: the case of Jane Wenham (1712)', *Eighteenth-Century Studies*, 15, 1981–82.

118   Harley, D., 'Historians as demonologists: the myth of the midwife-witch', *The Journal for the Social History of Medicine*, 3, 1990.

119   Hitchcock, J., 'George Gifford and Puritan witch beliefs', *Archiv für Reformationgeschichte*, 58, 1967.

120   Holmes, C., 'Popular culture? Witches, magistrates and divines in early modern England', in S.L. Kaplan (ed.), *Understanding Popular Culture: Europe from the Middle Ages to the Nineteenth Century*, Houton, Berlin, etc., 1984.

121   Holmes, C., 'Women, witnesses and witches', *Past and Present*, 140, 1993.

122   Jones, N., 'Defining superstitions: treasonous Catholics and the Act against witchcraft of 1563', in C. Carlton, R.L. Woods, M.L. Robertson and J.S. Block (eds), *States, Sovereigns & Society in Early Modern England: Essays in Honour of A.J. Slavin*, Sutton, 1998.

123   Kelly, H.A., 'English kings and the fear of sorcery', *Medieval Studies*, 39, 1977.

124   Larner, C., 'James VI and I and witchcraft', in A.G. Smith (ed.), *The Reign of James VI and I*, Macmillan, 1973.

125   Macfarlane, A., 'A Tudor anthropologist: George Gifford's *Discourse* and *Dialogue*', in S. Anglo (ed.), *The Damned Art: Essays in the Literature of Witchcraft*, Routledge and Kegan Paul, 1977.

126 Prior, M.E., 'Joseph Glanvill, witchcraft and seventeenth-century science', *Modern Philology*, 30, 1932.

127 Purkiss, D., 'Women's stories of witchcraft in early modern England: the house, the body, the child', *Gender and History*, 7, 1995.

128 Rushton, P., 'Women, witchcraft and slander in early modern England: cases from the church courts of Durham, 1560–1675', *Northern History*, 18, 1982.

129 Sawyer, R.C. ' "Strangely handled in all her lyms": witchcraft and healing in Jacobean England', *Journal of Social History*, 22, 1988–89.

130 Sharpe, J.A., 'Witchcraft and women in seventeenth-century England: some northern evidence', *Continuity and Change*, 6, 1991.

131 Sharpe, J.A., *Witchcraft in seventeenth-century Yorkshire: accusations and counter measures*, Borthwick Papers, 81, York, 1992.

132 Sharpe, J.A., 'Women, witchcraft and the legal process', in J. Kermode and G. Walker (eds), *Women, Crime and the Courts in Early Modern England*, University College London Press, 1994.

133 Sharpe, J.A., 'Disruption in the well-ordered household: age, authority and possessed young people', in P. Griffiths, A. Fox and S. Hindle (eds), *The Experience of Authority in Early Modern England*, Macmillan, 1996.

134 Swain, J.T., 'The Lancashire witch trials of 1612 and 1634 and the economics of witchcraft', *Northern History*, 30, 1994.

135 Teall, J.L., 'Witchcraft and Calvinism in Elizabethan England: divine power and human agency', *Journal of the History of Ideas*, 23, 1962.

136 Tyler, P., 'The church courts at York and witchcraft prosecutions, 1567–1640', *Northern History*, 4, 1970.

137 Unsworth, C.R., 'Witchcraft beliefs and criminal procedure in early modern England', in T.G. Watkins (ed.), *Legal Records and Historical Reality: Proceedings of the Eighth British Legal History Conference, Cardiff, 1987*, Hambledon Press, 1989.

C. Other Works Cited

138 Daly, M., *Gyn/ecology: the Metaethics of Radical Feminism*, Women's Press, 1979.

139 Geertz, H., 'An anthropology of religion and magic', *Journal of Interdisciplinary History*, 6, 1975.

140 Gough, R., *The History of Myddle*, ed. David Hey, Penguin Books, Harmondsworth, 1981.

141 Hutton, S. (ed.), *Henry More (1614–1687: Tercentenary Studies*, Kluwer Academic Publishers, Dordrecht, Boston and London, 1990.

142 Ingram, M.J., *Church Courts, Sex and Marriage in England, 1570–1640*, Cambridge University Press, Cambridge, 1987.

143 Lindley, D., *The Trials of Francis Howard: Fact and Fiction at the Court of King James*, Routledge, London and New York, 1993.

144 North, R., *The Lives of the Right Hon. Francis North, Baron Guildford, the Hon. Sir Dudley North, and the Hon. and Rev. Dr John North, together with the Autobiography of the Author*, ed. Augustus Jessop, 3 vols, 1890.

145 *The Rev. Oliver Heywood, B.A., 1630–1712. His Autobiography, Diaries, Anecdote and Event Books*, ed. J. Horsfall Turner, 4 vols, Brighouse, 1882–85.

146 Sharpe, J.A., *Defamation and Sexual Slander in Early Modern England: the Church Courts at York*, Borthwick Papers, 58, York, 1981.

147 Sharpe, J.A., *Early Modern England: a Social History 1550–1760*, 2nd edn, Arnold, 1997.

148 Sharpe, J.A., *Crime in Early Modern England 1550–1750*, 2nd edn, Longman, 1999.

149 *Somerset Assize Orders 1629–1640*, ed. T.G. Barnes, Somerset Record Society, 65, 1962.

150 Stone, L., *The Family, Sex and Marriage in England 1500–1800*, Weidenfeld and Nicolson, 1977.

151 Thomas, K., 'History and anthropology', *Past and Present*, 24, 1963.

152 *'William Holcroft his Booke': Local Office-holding in Late Stuart Essex*, ed. J.A. Sharpe (Essex Historical Documents, 2, Essex Record Office), Chelmsford, 1986.

153 Wrightson, K., 'The politics of the parish in early modern England', in A. Fox, P. Griffiths and S. Hindle (eds), *The Experience of Authority in Early Modern England*, Macmillan, 1996.

Index